Coming
HOME

A Travel Journal

Julie Maijala Lundquist

Published by: ADVANTAGE BOOKS™
www.advbookstore.com

Unless otherwise indicated, Bible quotations, unless otherwise noted, are from the New International Version of the Bible, copyright @ 1984 by the International Bible Study.

Library of Congress Control Number: 2007942110

Cover design by Pat Theriault

First Printing: December 2007
07 08 09 10 11 12 13   10 9 8 7 6 5 4 3 2 1
Printed in the United States of America

Dedication

For Alfred, my grandfather, and his great love for us.

Julie Maijala Lundquist

Acknowledgements

What a journey. I am so very thankful for all the guides God has placed in my life - family, friends, authors and yes, many strangers. Thank you Glenn for letting me in, asking good questions and creating space for me to listen. I am especially thankful for my husband Paul, whom I love dearly and my precious, precious children who live as bright beacons. For all of you that I have been blessed to walk beside, I am thankful. May these stories give you wings to fly.

Dear Marcia,

May your days
be filled with the
riches of beauty, love
and great joy.

Julie Lundquist

Table of Contents

Itinerary

Wild Geese

You do not have to be good.
You do not have to walk on your knees.
For a hundred miles through the desert repenting.
You only have to let the soft animal of your body
Love what it loves.
Tell me about despair, yours, and I will tell you about mine. Meanwhile
the world goes on.
Meanwhile the sun and clear pebbles of the rain
Are moving across landscapes,
Over the prairies and the deep trees,
The mountains and the rivers.
Meanwhile the wild geese, high in the clean blue air,
Are heading home again.
Whoever you are, no matter how lonely,
The world offers itself to your imagination,
Calls to you like the wild geese, harsh and exciting –
Over and over announcing your place
In the family of things.
Mary Oliver

By all accounts, my life has been pretty amazing. I was born in the spring of 1967 to two very interested and loving parents. I shared a close-knit family life with my sister. We were active at church, went to summer school, church camp, sang in the choir, played sports, excelled at school, laughed, fought and played. There was no doubt of God's presence in my life. I knew God loved me, Jesus died for me and my sins had been forgiven.

After college I married my high school sweet heart – one of my best friends since 7th grade. Talk about evidence of God's love for me. I married the man God had chosen to be my life partner. Life was so exciting. We had a beautiful wedding, got jobs – good ones, too – and built our first house. After four years of enjoying each other we knew we wanted to start a family. That came pretty easy and over the next few years we were blessed with three beautiful children, Megan, Mitchell and McKenzie Kaye. What miracles, I had no idea I would be so humbled by the many things they would teach me.

In the late 90's, Paul and I moved to be closer to my sister and her husband. Kari and Mike were expecting their first child and we knew we wanted to be closer to them. So, we built a house about 300 yards away from theirs. We were happy; Paul and I were doing well. He had a good job he loved, we had these beautiful children, I was living a stone's throw away from my sister and my dearest friends – but I was feeling so very alone. I couldn't shake it. I had been this nice obedient girl my whole life, was living a life so filled with success, was surrounded by people who loved and I still had this nagging feeling that would creep into my heart. I was so lonely. I couldn't figure it out.

I loved to travel and had been blessed with seeing God's grace and beauty all over the world. In all my trips, I never had felt this homesick, longing feeling. I was racked with guilt because I was homesick when I was here, in my own house. This feeling would sneak into my heart, like a lion waiting for darkness to pounce on its prey. So, being the first-born, self-motivated over achiever that I am, I decided to fix that problem. I got involved. I did a lot of doing – volunteering, scheduling play dates, teaching gardening courses, girl's night out, I ran my own photography studio. I wanted everyone to like me and I didn't want to ruffle anyone's feathers. I was so obedient to what our culture says a good wife and mother should be. You say 'jump' and I will ask how high – and usually give you even more. But still, at night after everyone had fallen asleep, I would lie in my bed and feel so empty.

Plain and simple, I was homesick. I had gotten so caught up in doing the right things, following the rules, being a nice person that I had built myself a prison cell. I couldn't get out and I was really struggling with this. I was living the life of the successful American dream and I was so thankful for everyone in my life – my husband, my family and friends, but there was this sliver of such sadness, such longing in my heart that I couldn't fill. Finally, I had enough. I gave it up. You see, in my heart of hearts, not the one that I had sold out and given to everyone else, but in my true heart I hadn't given God my whole life. Oh, I thought I was smart enough to give him the big chunks – my husband, my children, my family. But the other things – finances, friends, the small details in my day-to-day stuff? Well God, I was just fine. I liked being in control – besides, I was good at what I did.

But I was exhausted. I asked God to take it – all. I had been so afraid of doing this. I had been so afraid of asking God to carry me, of not wanting to lose control. But I gave my life to God – every last painful, lonely, glorious wonderful scrap of it. I prayed this while I was putting away laundry. I was surprised by how easy it was. But there was no lighting bolt, no "shazam." I was still breathing and I went on with my life. Nothing much changed on the outside but my faith was in motion again.

Journal

Set up road signs; Put up guideposts. Take note of the highway, the road that you take. Jeremiah 31:12

I have felt that I am on the cusp of something - but I am not sure what. Every morning I wake with anticipation and am encouraged by the voice in my head to write. It's like a mother encouraging a small child to go ahead and try something new, while leaving enough room for the child to choose. It is not a mandate but a grace filled compass directing me down a path. Perhaps I write in order to make sense of the roar I hear in my heart. Perhaps I write in hope of creating a map, claiming a territory, or simply to leave crumbs along the road so that if I get lost again, I can find my way back home.

Hand written words echo
Lifting a familiar voice I have known all my life
Like the vapor of rain
Hanging over scorched earth.

My words on blank pages pile up and form markers as I gain insight. These piles of words simply mark the way I have traveled. They are signposts of my journey of this great pilgrimage called life. I guess I leave these words on the page in trust and belief that there are other travelers out there. I trust I am not the only one on an amazing journey. May my words mark this journey as true. May these stories lift and encourage you.

Hard Work

When the Lord your God brings you into the land he swore to your fathers, to Abraham, Isaac and Jacob, to give you – a land with large flourishing cities you did not build, houses filled with all kinds of things you did not provide, wells you did not dig, and vineyards and olive groves you did not plant – then when you eat and are satisfied – be careful that you do not forget the Lord, who brought you out of Egypt, out of slavery. Deuteronomy 6:10

I'm the first-born child of a Finlander and the daughter of a woman whose family's great depression lasted much longer than American history defines. So hard work? You better believe it. Hard work has been part of our family motto since the beginning. I learned that hard work is nothing to scoff at and nothing to be afraid of. I am thankful for these two gifts my family passed along, but somewhere along the line I got things a little mixed up.

I got the "work" part mixed up in my faith life. You see, I thought that if I work hard here in the outside world, well then, you get noticed, you get paid, you get raises, you can feed your family. You can do anything. There I said it, I believed that with hard work I could do anything. I found myself alone out there with no room for anyone else besides a very small select few. More importantly, I had left very little room for God. I am so thankful that He never gave up on me.

God makes it so much simpler – and I choose the word simpler (not easy) because for me this lesson was (and is) still one of the hardest ones I have ever learned. It is not easy for me to stop orchestrating, planning every detail, scheming about what is going to happen next (are you getting a new picture of control freak?) But I got tired. I was absolutely exhausted.

In the midst of all this exhaustion, against all better judgment, I agreed to get a puppy. What was I thinking??? Our youngest child was beginning 1st grade, and for the first time in 10 years I would have a stretch of time with possibilities. Possibilities for me to be free! I would have a break. Strangely enough, I not only agreed to get a puppy, I really *wanted* to get a puppy. Call me crazy but in so many ways this dog, Rookie, was and is a big part of my faith walk. I believe that God can and does work through everything in our life to get our attention. I must be pretty pig headed and stubborn because I was sent this ever growing, ever consuming dog. I know that everyday God uses this beautiful world to guide and direct me.

Rookie

For we walk by faith, not by sight. 2 Corinthians 5:7

Rookie was a wild energetic puppy (we call him many things, one of which is "The Beast") and I walked him religiously two times a day. One slow moving, cool, damp spring morning we were walking our usual route – down past the elementary school, across the parking lot, around the big soccer fields, next to the road with the 6-foot cyclone fence. I was walking and noticing the moist air. I was on a path I had probably walked a couple hundred times. I knew every landmark, tree, fence, and speed limit sign. I knew where the sidewalk curved and where it went straight.

I could have walked that path with my eyes closed, but a strange thing happened. The wet spring air descended and a cloud of fog surrounded me. I had let the dogs off lead and they were running free. I looked up and realized I couldn't see a thing. I couldn't see the fence, the road, or the dogs. I held out my hand and I could barley even see it. That's when it hit me like a load of bricks. I realized believing is more than seeing. I realized I was so powerfully loved.

Peace came over me, clean and fresh like the water droplets landing on my cheeks and eye lashes. The water simply washed it all away. I don't even really know what the "it" was, but whatever it was, it had been really getting in my way of living my life to the potential God had intended. And I let it. I heard that all my effort and work had gotten me lost to the beauty and riches that God wanted for me in my life. In that one minute, it was if the skin that had been covering my eyes had been peeled off. There, on the sidewalk along County Road 16 I could see brilliantly for the first time in years.

The fog that had somehow limited my physical sight healed my soul and spirit. I could see. I came to realize that the work I must do is get out of the way. I must stop the craziness that I so often had created, rushing from here to there because I thought I must, or should, or had to. Jesus' message is simple – hard, but simple. Let go, let me wash you, I have come to love you. Let me. Let me wash you and renew your spirit. Let me hold you and love you and show you the way. Trust me, child. You are mine and I will carry anything for you. Just give it to me. There is no burden in my world. There is only light. Look for it wherever you go, name it. Encourage it. Lift up your neighbors. You are never alone. I love you.

How can it be that a simple ordinary walk with the dog could change my life? How can it be, that while standing in thick fog I could see perfectly for the first time in years? How can it be?

Camping

So I commend the enjoyment of life, because nothing is better for a man under the sun to eat and drink and be glad. Then joy will accompany him in his work all the days of the life God has given him under the sun. Ecclesiastes 8:15

Everyone who doesn't camp talks about how much work it is. I want to laugh – camping is easy. It cuts out all of the unnecessary garbage that fills my life. Living outdoors close to nature brings me back to the basics. Food, adequate shelter, layers of clothing and water are all we truly need. The "fun" of life is filled out here in nature with spirit and soul – creative imagination, adventure, sense of awe, intrigue, discovery and a desire to see and do what the heart calls for. No Internet, cell phones, telephones, TV or licking my paw about trivial issues. I wake each day simply to love the world and all that lives in it.

Perhaps camping teaches us true living. It teaches living by heart. You know how those songs you memorized by heart so long ago seem to surface years later at just the right moment? Or how after years of not riding a bicycle you can hop back on and go? I believe that living in Christ is truly living by heart. Living life to the fullest is living in rhythm to Christ in you and around you. Get out of the car, leave the "easy" life and explore – you may just find the place your heart and spirit have been searching for.

Perfection

You may say to yourself "My power and strength of my hands have produced this wealth for me." But remember the Lord your God, for it is HE who gives you ability to produce wealth and so confirms his covenant, which he swore to your forefathers, as it is today. Deuteronomy 8:17-18

I have spent much of my life trying to fulfill expectations of others –my parents, my husband, my friends and my neighbors. I didn't want to disappoint anyone, I wanted to fit the bill of what everyone needed, but it wasn't working. I so often pretended like I could do it all, that I had it all under control. I juggled so much, tried to be the perfect wife, mother, daughter and friend that you could ever want. I often acted like my energy was unlimited and I gave and gave and gave. I gave so much that I often felt numb.

I didn't know how hard I was being on myself. I didn't realize how important it was for me to make time to spend with myself. I didn't know how important it was to rest and dwell in the land that I had been given. If I ever did slow down, I felt so much guilt. I knew I was missing something vital to life, but I couldn't find my way out. I didn't realize that every time I tried to act like the perfect daughter, wife, sister, friend it was all about building up my own ego. I didn't realize that so much of my giving was done to satisfy my pride. I wasn't able to rest because I was afraid if I did you might not like me. I had a long way to fall. I realized that I was failing on all sides. I was overwhelmed with the burden of trying to be perfect. I couldn't hold it up anymore.

My road to freedom was found when I realized I didn't have to be perfect. I realized that all my trying had carried me so far away from God and everything true living was about. I needed to realize that I was not in charge of the universe. I needed to learn that it is God who makes us perfect through his gracious love. I needed to learn how to love myself. I needed to remember how to let go and live by heart.

Peace

Not a place. Not a feeling.
It is the engagement between me and something else
It is hope and belief I am not alone.
It is being in community with everything around us.

Paul and I spent a weekend away in Seattle. He had to travel there on business in the city and I was bent on getting out of dodge into the peaceful and quiet countryside. I was hungry for peace. After his meetings, we jumped into our sporty economy rental car in search of peace, fleeing the traffic, the noise and hustle. I was certain a rural setting would calm my restlessness. As we traveled through the San Juan Islands, a place of surreal beauty, I saw glimpses of beauty, but no peace. We marveled at the new landscapes, soaked in the ambiance of the islands and enjoyed the trip, but I did not find what I was looking for.

It was not until we returned to the city on Sunday night that peace found me. I find it so strange that I insisted on getting out of the city and into the country for peace and relaxation only to return and have *it* find *me* in the totally crowded noise filled streets of the city.

Peace is not a location; it is a place in the heart. It is opening oneself up to the beauty of the moment, exactly where you are. Peace is in the details, not in the landscape. Admiring leaf prints stained into the cement along sidewalks, feeling the stone inlay of a beautiful hand carved wooden chair in the bustling market of Seattle, sitting with Paul in the hotel lobby and interrupting each other with comments from our books, enjoying the warmth of his hands on my cold ones, walking past shops with no interest, sleeping in and making love to music, laughing out loud at the movie theatre, walking all over town, feeling the cold wet rain on my face, and allowing myself to simply be. Peace is being open to God's presence with all of my heart, soul, mind and body. Ask and the door will be opened, seek and you will find.

Cancer

*Hear O Lord, and answer me, For I am poor and needy. Guard
my life, for I am devoted to you. You are my God; Save your
servant who trusts in you. Have mercy on me O Lord, For I call
on you all day long. Bring joy to your servant, For to you, O Lord,
I lift up my soul. Psalm 86:1-4*

Do you remember the first time you said a really bad swear word? Do you
remember how it felt? How it tasted? I don't remember which bad word I said
first but I remember thinking that it would make me feel strong and tough. It
didn't. It made me feel small and powerless.

There is a new swear word in my vocabulary. My Dad called with the
results of his biopsy and as he said the word cancer my body crumpled to the
kitchen floor. He is the rock in our family, our stable compass. How could this
happen? How could my Daddy have cancer? This word cancer holds that same
awful taste in my mouth like a swear word does. I feel powerless, small and very,
very scared. But at the same time that simple word has created a new awareness
– like the shock you feel when you plummet off the high point of a rollercoaster
and then the realization that this too, is part of the ride. Dad's cancer has created a
sieve into which my life has dropped. What is this that is trying to take my
already rich life (wasn't I just beginning to find it?) and drop it into the black
hole? But the miracle? The cradle, the sieve, God's grace, allowed all the
unimportant junk to fall through the holes. I am left with a new awareness of the
majesty of life.

My life doesn't seem changed as in putting in a new light bulb; instead it is
richer and more pure, filled with grace and love. It is thicker, deeper, and more
dimensional. I think that it was always there before, but daily living had dirtied
up the furniture – and I saw the dust, not the beauty there standing strong. The
last few weeks have taken my lettuce leaf life and tossed it into the colander –
leaving my life clean, moist, pure, and crisp – desired.

Cairn

I can do everything through him who gives me strength.
Philippians 4:12-13

It's early morning and I awake a little after sunrise. The light is so sweet, soft golden warm with a hint of red orange. It is amazing. I haven't been sleeping well the past few weeks. Dad hasn't started his chemo – it has been another cycle of hurry up and wait. I am scared things are worse than we thought. Dad heard he might be slated for "research treatment." My stomach gets tied up in knots and fear moves in. I am really fighting it. I pray for help for my family and me. I pray for healing. I pray for peace. I think Mom and Dad are scared, I know Kari is – and we just can't go there. Fear chokes all truth and no one speaks about the silent swear words we hear being shouted all over our home.

And then I read:

Nothing is more valuable than this day. Goethe

And that is what I hold onto. I choose to stop fighting and cling to the truth.

Iraq

Let us not become weary in doing good, for at the proper time we will reap a harvest if we do not give up. Therefore, as we have opportunity, Let us do good to all people. Galatians 6:9

We attacked Iraq last week beginning a whole new war. Now this is horror. The media is right there and the television virtually invites the atrocities of war right into our family room. Words like "Sadam Hussein, Iraq, Kuwait, land mine, mortar" and "dead" roll off my children's tongues with strange familiarity and boldness. These are smart children, aware and in tune. I have always promised to be truthful with answers to their questions. Where in the world do they come up with such insightful questions? "Mommy, if Sadam Hussein asks for forgiveness, will he go to heaven?" "Why would someone WANT to crash a plane into a building?" "You mean they tried to?"

On a world map, Iraq seems to be an incomprehensible distance away. But in the map of our lives the people there are our neighbors. All of our children are too young to lose their innocence. Dear God, forgive us, lead us and guide us.

Where is your fish?

See, I have engraved you on the palms of my hands; Your walls are ever before me. Isaiah 49:15-16

It is not surprising in such a material name brand world that some folks have decided to brand the Christian way of life in the shape of the ancient fish. Check it out. The fish is everywhere - on necklaces, sweatshirts, t-shirts and on the back of cars. Perhaps this marketing phenomenon began as witness, discipleship or evangelism – but it seems to have evolved into a measurement of faith. If you don't display this symbol (logo) – then you are not enough. The fish has created an exclusive club. You want in? Then you need to dress like us, worship like us, vote like us, educate like us and your automobile has to prominently display the fish on its rear.

Think about it. We have taken a symbol used during the ancient times of Christian persecution and marketed it into a symbol of elitism. Have the requirements for the entry into the kingdom of God gotten longer? Our current culture seems to have created specs outlining the admission to become a child of God. We seem to have become obsessed with 'perfection" and have forgotten that Christ's death on the cross paid our admission. We are debt free. It is only through God's grace that we can truly experience the Christian life. It is not something we earn.

What ever happened to "they will know we are Christians by our love"? Where is your fish? Embed it in your heart, let it live in your mind and flow from your lips. God's love sets us free, as we are, to live as children of God. Christ set us free to be individuals, utilizing our unique gifts. We have been called as his children to light the world – so that we may be the hands and feet of Christ.

Julie Maijala Lundquist

Antennae

People talk for hours
And never really speak.
People listen
And never really hear.
What did you say?

Picture this: imagine flying over the city and instead of satellite dishes and TV antennae out on the roofs, the people are out on roofs, on streets, living with arms stretched, palms lifted towards heaven. Instead of creating chaos in our lives to fill the void, we patiently wait and listen. We wait with the attitude of being open, trusting that God is at work right where we are. We simply live while giving praise and thanksgiving to God for his marvelous works of glory each and every day.

Imagine a nation full of people who aren't afraid to turn off their cell phones, who don't run to the phone because they might miss something, but instead is tuned in and listening with our hearts. Imagine trusting that what is happening every minute and even this very second, right in front of you, is where you have been called. Imagine the peace. Imagine the power. Imagine the love.

Travels

608 Court, Adel Iowa

Time passes, travel is long.
Stiff and awkward I stumble out of the passenger seat.
Sneakers slide, fight for footing on gravel.
One step at a time I make my way towards the light.

The big house hovers, gentle and friendly
White paint peeling, front porch wraps 'round, welcoming.
Windows, bright like beacons, glow
Pouring out honey through white gauze curtains
Swaying from side to side.

Small town crickets sing a big city chorus
While moths flicker like angels, repel off glass,
Waiting.
I am wide-awake and the front door opens
I step inside heaven.

Voices clamor in welcoming rhythms of aunts, uncles and cousins
And the scent of supper lingers
Like an aphrodisiac for the homesick.
Floors slant, chairs creak, couches sag
Worn with memories of bodies that rest here
While framed faces of loved ones float on walls.

It's no catalog layout or glossy photo from House Beautiful
It is love and life, worn and familiar, the story of living.
My heart sings.
I am home.

I have been homesick. Homesick for heaven. How foreign that idea seems, but it is true. This longing has brought me on many travels all over the world. I am blessed to have seen so many slices of heaven on earth. In places such as Acadia, Black Hills, quiet meandering streams outside of Yellowstone, sunset in the Grand canyon, Nanbojou, Captiva, Madeline Island and the BWCA my soul feels free. I feel at home.

I have so often felt a yearning to stay in these places – to make them my home, away from hustle and bustle of the world. I have so wrongly believed that I had to move or travel great distances to find home. I know how to be at home traveling around the world. Now I want to learn how to be home under my own roof.

Love in motion

Let me not listen
With ears of this world.
Teach me to listen
With my whole soul.

Cleanse my heart
With gentle lapping of water,
Softening stone.

Help me listen to the silence
Of Your Greatness
Of Your Wholeness
Of Your Completeness.

Drain the noise from my human ears
And let your spirit cleanse me
As the waters flow.

I have a natural tendency for motion – running, gardening, artistry, traveling, teaching, sweating. Motion is a way my physical self communes with my soul. It is as if sweat and motion lubricate the boundary between spirit and self, between soul and body and allows for communication to occur between the two. When I am moving I can feel my spirit in the palm of my hands as well as within the palm of my heart.

Running in 90-degree heat, I am thankful for motion and the methodical pulse of my heartbeat, cleansing my body as it sweats out impurities. Grime rolls off my soul leaving me refreshed and cleansed. My thoughts are slow and audible as I run and I hear the voice I have known all my life. For so long I have heard without listening. I tuned out because I was afraid. I was afraid of what "giving it all up to God" might really mean. I was afraid of what God would want from me – maybe I wouldn't be good enough, or worthy enough, or just plain enough. I have been afraid I couldn't do it (whatever God wanted) by myself. I think I missed the point. I was never meant to do it by myself. We are meant to live this life *with* God.

I pray God uses me in this body of mine. I pray my soul is unleashed. I pray for the gift of healing so that I may help those around me. I pray I will not be afraid to use my gifts. I pray others will see my body is not who I am. I pray that grace, love and generosity may reside within me and resonate through its every pore. I pray that with every breath I take I will resolve to be open to the powers of the spirit so I may be used here on earth. I know I am a part of Gods plan. I am ready and willing. I feel no fear. I feel only love and the glowing warmth that rests in my heart.

100% Satisfaction

We are caught in the current of life
Drowning while holding on
Afraid of being pulled into the stream
Gasping for air, having forgotten to Let Go

Wake up. Notice the water
As it caresses our nakedness
Give life and we soar.

Our lives don't come with a guarantee of 100 % satisfaction. Life in Christ doesn't promise perfection. He promises a lifeline as we struggle through dips and valleys, climb up hills and saunter along plains. The satisfaction of life comes out of its joy – its beauty and its hardships. It is knowing that our hands are never empty because Christ always holds them in our walk of life.

Is 100% satisfaction ever possible? Can it be found anywhere on earth without the love of Christ? Perhaps the glitz and shimmer of new objects woo us. Possessions may temporarily transform the landscape of our faces into wide mouthed grins – but it is fleeting at best. The truth, the joy, the smile felt in the heart is found by looking through Christ's eyes and seeing the beauty and wonders of this world – and thanking God for the miracle of life and love. I have found truth in Christ. There is 100% satisfaction after all.

Rain

Are we afraid?
Only willing to stand inside,
Face pressed to glass
And watch the drops fall?

Water falls from heaven
Cleansing leaves,
Nourishing dry parched earth,
Soaking in,
Quenching thirst.

But we stand inside, worried.
Maybe we will get wet
or cold
or look foolish.

Too afraid to step outside
We hunch our shoulders,
Jump over puddles
And run as fast as we can
To avoid getting wet.

Everyday there is a chance of rain. Why does it seem when the rains come we act as if we will melt if the water falls on us? Why are we so afraid of rain, only willing to stand inside, face pressed against the glass, watching the rainfall? Embrace the rain, it is so renewing. Tears are such a key in healing. Allowing myself to listen and hear God stirred up the Holy Spirit and loosened my heart. The tears flowed and I found the lost language of our culture - the language of love.

I had built myself a glass prison cell and I had no idea I was building one. The walls were high and so carefully, slowly erected over time that I never even realized I was looking through glass. I was missing the view. I never realized that I was no longer free. It had happened so slowly that I didn't even know I was trapped in ego and pride. I desperately didn't want to disappoint anyone. I wanted to be well liked, well respected. I wanted to be right. I had so often become what everyone else wanted me to be, I totally lost sight of who God wanted me to be. I forgot who God had created me to be.

Through grace the rains came and the spirit softened my heart. In the Old Testament, Jeremiah tells the story of God's sadness when he sees what has happened to his marvelous creation. God calls out to the women and asks them to announce the change in the world. God calls for the wailing women. God calls to the women to take action. God calls to us and tells us to get our faces wet. Tears are often the first step in healing this wounded creation. Tears bring growth. Tears announce change. Tears are the prelude to joy. Dear Lord, I cry for the imprisoned. Put me to work. I am ready to be your change in this world.

Prodigal daughter

But while he was still a long way off, his father saw him and was filled with compassion for him; he ran to his son, threw his arms around him and kissed him. Luke 15:20

I always thought I was more like the "good" son who stayed at home and worked in the fields. I identified with the older son who had worked all those years not disobeying orders. But the orders I was following were not God's – they were my own. I gave all my freedom away trying to be obedient to the box our culture put me in.

I always thought about the rules first because I didn't want to be wrong. I didn't want to get in trouble. My need to be right stopped so much love from flowing out. Heck, it stopped God's love from flowing in. I was raised not to question authority and I gave away my authority to everyone except the One to whom it belonged.

What I realize now is I am the prodigal daughter returning home after years of hiding behind the perfect 2-story home. I am returning home after squandering so much of the blessings I have been given. Now I find myself turning around and running for home.

I was living a kind of walking death. When I look back I see that I spent so much time sleepwalking. I had a good life, I smiled, I laughed, and I loved. I was happy but I had kept parts of my life away from God. I often saw my life as game pieces of Trivia Pursuit and I figured I was a good enough player to keep some of the pieces of the pie for myself. Since I had given God most of the pieces, it couldn't hurt if I held on to some of the others. Besides, I had done a pretty good job on my own. But so often I was filled with worry, anxiety and guilt. It would hit me like a punch in the gut at night when I lay down to sleep and I would lay awake for hours, stomach tied in knots, trying to figure it out.

I was the woman who invited chaos into her house in order to hide her talents. I was the woman who wanted to be nice; I wanted people to like me. Now I am learning that being nice is all about <u>not</u> breaking the rules,

<u>not</u> talking back, <u>not</u> making waves, <u>not</u> allowing anyone not to like you. It's a tough climate to grow in, this climate of not. I have learned that God isn't calling us to be nice. He is calling us to great. God is calling us to be great women who live in goodness, doing and being out of love.

I kept myself locked in prison based upon the cultural expectations of what I thought I should do in order to be a nice girl. My home was my prison. I was locked in "self" and I was all alone. I got stuck there because I never told my stories – I never shared my struggles or my joy. I hid and so often got caught up in telling every one else's story that I forgot I had one to share. I believe we are created to share our struggles and rejoice in the richness of our lives that God has given each one of us. I have learned that we must share both joy and pain not to find answers, but to build community and struggle together. I have learned when we shift our focus from our struggles to God's great love and compassion miracles happen.

I learned what I "possessed" got in the way of letting my light shine, of being my true self. I possessed material things, my husband, my house, and my children. Shopping was something "real" or so I thought, that could provide me with things to help fill the void. This "stuff" helped to create the walls of my prison. It got in the way of allowing me to love others and to trust them. I had a lot of possessions. I realize now that the more things we hold on to, the more likely we are to remain locked in prison. Possessions get in the way – they block light and the spirit of love.

I think a miracle happened. Acts of the Holy Sprit are being repeated in the lives of ordinary people daily, and I am one of them. The breath of the Holy Spirit shattered my glass house and I found myself outside on the road back home. I am coming home, back to the child of God I was created to be. My story is the story of love in motion. My story is the story of God in my life each and every day, the story of freedom. Instead of adding to the image I carried of myself, I am learning by moving, physically, mentally and spiritually, I experience the paring down of my rough exterior only to find beauty beneath.

Julie Maijala Lundquist

Threshold

We look with uncertainty
Beyond the old choices for
Clear cut answers
To a softer, more permeable aliveness
Which is every moment
At the brink of death;
For something new is being born in us
If we but let it.
We stand at a new doorway,
Awaiting that which comes…
Daring to be human creatures,
Vulnerable to the beauty of existence.
Learning to love.
-Anne Hillman

So often I stood in the threshold of my heart. You know the place at the edge of the entrance, neither in nor out? Not moving? I was stuck and had a hard time letting anyone new in this heart of mine. I didn't invite many in. If I did, I am so sorry – I had forgotten how to be a friend. I held most of my relationships out on the front porch – often times with the door opened just a crack, but rarely invited anyone in. I stood in the threshold, too afraid of disappointing you with what you would find on the inside.

I didn't want to show my weaknesses. I was afraid of making true friends. It might be too painful, and besides someone (me) might get hurt. Sure, I might have invited you over for a proper tea, but I was usually guarded. My heart would hide below the surface and I would pull the curtains tight, just barley peeking through the crack. Most of my relationships were merely held on the surface of my heart. I attended my share of Bunko games and Pampered Chef parties but I really shared little of me, and I was so lonely.

Behind the walls, I had forgotten who I was. I had forgotten how to really love myself. I felt unworthy, stupid and not enough. I was stuck because I was unwilling to accept the fact that it IS all about me. Living is all about living as the child God created me to be. Living is all about being free to be who we are, just as we are – and trusting that God loves us today and tomorrow. He loves us so much that he wants us to continue to move and grow. It's not about finishing the race; it is all about purely living every step of the way. God tore the curtain in hope that would we know there was nothing to hide from. God tore the curtain so we would see the light and life worth living.

Nakedness

Do not conform any longer to the pattern of this world, but be transformed by the renewing of your mind. Then you will be able to test and approve what God's will is – his good, pleasing and perfect will. Romans 12:1-2

Like many kids in the 70's, I grew up in a house where most things were kept private. Everything personal was to be hidden. Show no weakness. Show no strength. What we talked about at the family dinner table was to stay there. We didn't want our dirty laundry hung out for all to see. But I saw that Adam and Eve hid in the garden, too. After they ate the forbidden fruit, fear set in and they realized that they were naked and vulnerable. They hid from God because they felt unworthy. I realized that I had been feeling unworthy, too.

I had separated myself from God and others. Even in our nakedness- or is it <u>in</u> our nakedness, God takes us in and loves us whole and complete. It is a matter of trusting God. He promises to love you. Sometimes it is not until our laundry is hung outside on the line that the wind blows through and the sun whitens our robes again. Sometimes, it's not until we hang our own stories on the line that we can actually see how bright some of the whites are illuminated by grace they become light for others.

Relief

Guard your steps when you go to the house of God. Go near to listen rather than offer the sacrifice of fools, who do not know what they do wrong. Ecclesiastes 5:1

By questioning where I stood, I moved. Questions led to answers, answers led to truth and truth always led to God. God provided me with questions – and answers. To know God is to listen and that was something that I had to learn to do all over again.

Have you ever had water stuck in your ear after swimming? You know that strange plugged up feeling? Listening to anything is distorted, uncomfortable and frustrating. Hearing God again was like the relief the moment water gets unstuck from your ear and drains out, running down your cheek.

Sacred

He put a new song in my mouth, a hymn of praise to our God. Many will see and hear and put their trust in the Lord. Psalm 40:3

Our everyday world is where the sacred is. God is everywhere and in everyone I meet. I am beginning to understand how very much I am loved – and how much God loves every other person. Everyday, every evening, every moment is new through God.

Naps

I will lie down and sleep in peace, for you alone, O Lord, make me dwell in safety. Psalm 4:8

I have never have been able to nap. Maybe it would be more true to say I rarely allowed myself to nap. Oh, I permitted a few winks here and there on some occasions. I napped outside at my friend's cabin, sleeping bags spread out across the lawn under warm summer skies. They were rich and refreshing. My soul relaxed and suddenly there was space for moving and breathing. Just remembering them fills me with such gratitude. I felt safe napping while camping or vacationing, but at home I never napped. I was too afraid I would miss out on something. I was too afraid I wouldn't be able to save the world.

No Regrets

But above all, my brothers, do not swear either by heaven or by earth or with any other oath: But your yes is to be yes, And your no, no So that you may not fall under judgment. Jas 5:12

My way of living used to be about saying yes to everything. I didn't believe that "no" was even part of living (unless of course it was stupidly dangerous). I was living completely outside of myself. I held tight to the motto "No Regrets" which meant I was afraid to miss out on anything. I didn't listen to what my heart really wanted. I figured I should try everything.

But truly living a "No Regrets" life is different because it is all about trusting your heart completely. It means believing Christ dwells within us and we must listen to our heart for guidance. It means having to say no sometimes, without any regret. It sometimes means saying no because in my heart, soul and whole being I know that God's plan for my life takes time to unfold. I can't run around trying to fix it, scheme it or plan it all myself. No regrets really is about being fully present to this very minute, and not missing out on any of the glorious amazing parts – even naps. It means listening with my soul and spirit as to what my heart yearns for. It is trusting Christ is truly within us and he will indeed guide us.

Renewed Truths of Abundance

We now serve not by following a set of rules but out of renewed hearts and minds that overflow with love for God.

Follow your heart.
Give God your heart and follow him.

Dance like no one's watching
God wants to be your partner for all life's dances.

It's not about you.
It really is about us (me and God, me and you, me and you and God).

Live every day like it's your last.
Live every day like it is your first – experience awe and excitement in every moment.

Everything you say can and will be used against you in a court of law.
Everything you say can and will transform you and every life around you.

Follow the rules and you will be safe.
Follow Jesus and you will experience amazing adventures.

Be the best that you can be.
Be the beautiful child of God you are.

Lock your doors and windows for protection.
Open your door wide and let the spirit in.

If you build it they will come.
Empty it and he will come.

Orienteering

Finally brothers, whatever is true, whatever is noble, hatever is right, whatever is pure, whatever is lovely, whatever is admirable – if anything is excellent or praiseworthy – think about such things. Philippians 4:8

I was orienteering with a group of 5th grade students and so often they went off course. They forgot which arrow they were supposed to follow. It was frustrating because we had to constantly remind them to get past their desire to follow North, the bright red arrow, instead of the clear directional arrow. The directional arrow, the one to really follow, is so much harder to see.

Have we taught our children to look for bright and colorful things for guidance and direction? Have we taught them to rely on commercials and billboards instead of trusting their heart? Have we forgotten to teach them to look for the truth of their own life? Finding our way, in orienteering and living, is about following our directional arrow, the direction of our hearts.

Northern Lights

An angel called in the night
To tell me about the light
"Get up" said she
"Go out and see"
But I stood in the shadow of doubt
And the darkness bid me not go out
The thought of wind
The threat of cold
Kept me from the glories foretold.
Yet still she's calling out to me
Undoubted in God's glory
From without "come out"
From within "Go forth"
The skies are dancing in the north!
The skies are dancing in the north!
-Kara Millerhagen

Have you ever seen them, the Northern Lights? They are breathtaking and amazing!! One summer night Paul and I were sitting in the backyard and we couldn't help but notice the flashing lights in the northern sky. At first we thought that it must be searchlight advertising the nearby casino, but then we saw changing colors light up the entire northern sky. We made several phone calls to our friends and family to tell them to get outside and experience the beauty for themselves.

As we made our calls we were often told "We have already seen them." I couldn't believe it. No one had called and told us to look! No one had to called to share this amazing joy. I can't imagine not sharing the story of the marvel, beauty and awe of God's creation. I want everyone to know how amazing this world is. I can't imagine not telling the story and encouraging people I love – and all of God's people to open their eyes and see. I couldn't go one more minute without saying, "LOOK!" "WAKE

UP" "You've got to see what God has done today, is doing today, right this very minute. What a treasure to be able to share this joy with others!

Can you imagine the change in this world if we didn't rush to the phone to report the latest crime, gossip, or ask "Did you see Oprah today?" But instead called each other with excited breathlessness about what God had done in our lives that very day?

Lost Language

The heavens declare the glory of God; The skies proclaim the work of his hands. Day after day they pour forth speech; Night after night they display knowledge. There is no speech or language where their voice is not heard. Their voice goes out into all the earth, Their words to the end of the world. Psalm 19:1-4

The lost language isn't nouns and verbs, stories or speech patterns; it is God's truth. It is the language we so rarely hear spoken in our world. The lost language of love can be written or spoken, sung, played on the violin or guitar, it can be found in the hum of the lawn mower or the laughter of children. It is encouragement, faith, hope, joy and peace. Oh, we might hear it on rare occasions, Sundays, weddings and the like. Perhaps we save the lost language like my Grandma saved candles, new towels and linens – something to be treasured – stored away in the closet, saving it for the "right" occasion. We can't afford to keep it stored any longer. Unlike things of this world, if love is kept we lose it all. It is precious only when we open the door and use it daily with everyone that we meet. We must spend it everywhere, at all times and in all places.

Love is resonance, the reflection between two beings communicating out of truth, building community. It is vibration, joy, light, peace, and laughter. It is inviting Jesus into our hearts, allowing him to love us and loving him so very much that we can't help but overflow with love for others. It is the language of building the kingdom, of fulfilling God's dream for his people. This lost language is vital to our map of living and without it the treasure will always remains buried. Without daily use it sits in the storeroom of our heart gathering dust, only to become some forgotten treasure unearthed long after we die. Have we lived when our children ask themselves as they clean our cupboards for the estate sale, "What on earth was she saving this for? It is absolutely beautiful!"

The Dream

In the beginning God created the heavens and the earth. Genesis 1:1

Our son Mick awoke one morning excited about his dream. He dreamt about a little girl crying, asking why isn't God in church anymore? In his dream, Mick opened his eyes and saw God. He looked and looked and all he could see anywhere and everywhere was God. Mick was not afraid. He comforted the girl and told her God is everywhere at once – in church, the depths of the ocean, at home, in the trees and everywhere you are. He was so sure of God and so sure that mere walls of church cannot contain God. Mick told her that sometimes we are just so close to God we can't see him.

Boxes

Then he carved all the walls of the house round about with carved engravings of cherubim, palm trees, and open flowers, inner and outer sanctuaries. 1 King 6:29

I think of the word box and immediately get claustrophobic. "Don't box me in", "think outside the box" and "don't get stuck in the box." I can't stand being confined or told that I can't do something that I am passionate about. I have always rooted for the underdog and done things the unconventional way. I have labeled boxes as "bad" and have often struggled with being placed in one. But I am learning that at times boxes can be a great way for God to give us a glimpse of his awesomeness. The peace and joy of Christ that surpasses all human understanding does just that – it surpasses all my human understanding. Sometimes I need a box to catch just a little bit of that grace so I can see it and experience it.

Sometimes a box holds a treasure just long enough so we can minutely comprehend God's teachings. The danger occurs when boxes become fences to permanently hold something in or out. The danger occurs when we think we can keep the truth confined within walls. Maybe the true purpose of a box is to be an empty vessel that only holds something for a short time. Maybe I need some boxes in my life to help me get a clue.

Safe

Like a horse in open country, they did not stumble; Like cattle that go down to the plain, they were given rest by the Spirit of the Lord. This is how you guided your people to make for yourself a glorious name. Isaiah 63:13-14

One foggy, dreary morning I was out for a run. I was running a small loop that took me from my house, past a nearby pasture, back around Community Park and then home again. I settled into my run and was listening. The air was soupy and the colors all around me were fuzzy tints of gray. The air was cool and my breath came out in puffs, floating and trailing off in short little wisps.

As I ran past a large six-foot fence enclosing the pasture, I noticed a rapid movement and bursts of hot breath rising into the air. I scrambled up to the top of a little embankment and looked through the cyclone fence. My heart jumped. I was face to face with a deer, I don't know who was more startled, and I could feel the hot breath of this six-point buck on my face. He had been frantically running, stuck in this pasture. He ran through the herd of cows, looking for an escape but the cows were most undisturbed by this beast frantically sprinting up and down the pasture, they simply continued to graze and let their eyes slowly wander as they watched him bolt through the land. I could tell by the wild look in his eyes he was frightened. We studied each other for a sliver of time before he fled, cutting to the right and then the left, as he continued to look for a way to escape.

I jogged back down the hill and began to pray. I felt so badly for the deer, he was STUCK. He was stuck inside this fence with cows. He was all alone. I prayed he might find a way to escape. I knew how it felt to be stuck. I knew how it felt to have no options, nowhere to turn. Dear God, show him the way out. The deer was strong, I had seen him run and he was graceful and swift. I prayed for him to be strong enough to jump over the fence and be free. I prayed as I ran. And as I ran I was making tracks to the other end of the pasture.

As I rounded the corner on the opposite side of the pasture, my heart sank in horror as I saw a man in camouflage. He wore a blaze orange vest and hunting hat and he was holding up a rifle aiming at something in the distance. He was aiming the gun at the pasture on the other side of the fence. I abruptly stopped my prayer and for the first time in my life I realized how safe a box can be. I realized that right now, the safest place for that beautiful strong amazing animal was in the fence.

I began to think; perhaps the cows slowly chewing their cud, simply living in the green pasture may have been looking at that deer wondering what all the fuss was about. I realized that so often I had been like that deer- running away, sprinting to the right and then to the left, wanting OUT! In just those few moments I remembered that I had so often wanted out of what God had wanted to give me. I saw I had been at war with God over my life. I saw that I had been arguing with God and by golly, I was not going to be some penned up animal.

But seeing that deer that morning taught me a lesson. There is much more freedom in the temple (the box) of God than anywhere else on earth. As a matter of fact, living in that very temple (box) would save my life. It would give me true freedom, just like the fence around the pasture would indeed save this deer.

Trust

Trust in the Lord with all your heart, and lean not on your own understanding. In all your ways acknowledge Him and he shall keep your path straight. Proverbs 3:5

It was a brilliant winter's day and the sun was shinning in the bright blue Minnesota sky. All around birds were singing and rejoicing in the rays of sun, their calls echoing joyfully as the sun warmed the snow. Melting snow fell off bare branches played a faint drumbeat ...the very beginning rhythm of spring.

I walked through the woods, noticing how very close the branches of the sumac trees were. I was thinking how very full and dense this space would be this summer. The bare trees would fill out and block most of the summer light from shinning through. As I made my way over a knoll, I noticed a thin clearing in the brush. I walked towards it and found myself on a thin path, just on the edge of the trees. One side of the path was open and airy, filled with large uniform cedars breathing their fresh minty scent into the air. On the other side, the woods were wild with dormant plant life; branches and vines grew chaotically over and around each other, their branches entangled in a wild forest of enchantment.

As I followed the path further into the woods I had to stoop. The delicate steps of a creature much smaller than me had worn a beautiful path that meandered through the woods. The path was fairly straight and simple, yet it flowed with grace like that of a kittens tail. I followed along the path along the edge of a ravine and came upon a clearing. There the sun shone so warmly and pure, I was certain I was on holy ground.

I stopped and stood straight, lifting my face to the very sun that warmed the earth. I was overcome with peace and joy and thanksgiving. I bowed my head to take a deep breath and opened my eyes. There in front of me was an amazing sight - two beautiful foxes. Even at the end of winter these animals were absolutely gorgeous. No skin and bones here, they had been living off the fat of the land all winter. Their coats were a thick auburn, the color of wealth and royalty.

One of them was standing and looking straight at me. She was not moving but really looking. It was as if she recognized me – or *knew* me – and knew not to be afraid. Her lively dark eyes looked straight into my very heart, acknowledging my presence. We both stood there, still–as if we were honoring one other. Finally, she turned around and slowly sauntered into her den. It was unreal. It was if she wanted me to know she was home and all was well. I was amazed she chose to stay. She chose not to hide or to run, but purely to stay.

As she entered her den, I was able to shift my gaze to the other fox. She was sleeping curled up in a little ball in one of the bright shafts of sunlight. She seemed to be basking in the warmth, content. I could hear my nephew calling from a long way off "Where are you?" Not wanting him to worry, I took a careful step towards his voice, but it wasn't careful enough. I heard the snap of the twig at the same time the sleeping fox did. She awoke and without looking she stood and bolted straight into the woods, running far away from her home. I watched her go, disappearing into the forest.

I stopped and thought about how opposite the actions of the two foxes were. One stayed put, trusting. The other trusted instinct to keep her safe and she ran, body flying down the hillside on grey legs. I took one final look at the clearing and walked back towards my nephew. It struck me how right both actions had been. It was right for the fox to stay put. It was right for the fox to run. I was again reminded of the abundance of right choices we can make. I was reminded about the importance of trusting my heart. I was reminded of how important it is to pay attention to the details, to live wholly and completely alive using all of our senses and following our heart.

You Are Welcome

"Thank you." "No, problem," we respond. What ever happened to "You're welcome"? As a parent, I have appointed myself as squadron leader of the manner police. "Say please and thank you. Don't forget, what do you say?" I say it so often it has made me think, what is my response when someone says 'thank you" to me? More often than not, it has been "No problem." But I think that my response is a very big problem indeed. What ever happened to "you are welcome?"

What does the word welcome mean? It says "Come in, I've opened the door; I want you here, you are important to me. Come again, make yourself at home, be yourself. I am willing to receive you." I think in the broader, truer sense it means that I understand the value of BOTH giving and receiving. "You are welcome," says that I want to be in true community with you, growing closer and closer to God along the way.

If we are called to live a Christ centered life, can you imagine not telling people they are welcome? Can you imagine thanking God for blessings in your life and hearing him say "no big deal, no sweat off my back, it was nothing"? I believe God's presence is indeed a big deal. I believe God works through every one of us – and that our only response is one of gratitude. You are welcome, please come again.

Born Again

"The wind blows wherever it pleases.
You hear its sound but you cannot tell where it comes from
or where it is going." John 3:8

Are there layers like an onion peel to being born again? I believe we are all born again and again in Christ. When Christ lives in our heart, when he has been wholly and completely invited there every morning, every minute is a new day. So once again, over and over we are born into Christ' love. So, born again? Absolutely. Not once, but every day (hopefully) for the rest of my life. I can't tell you why or how – only that what my intellect has believed to be true, my heart and life now know. Life is fresh and new – not like it was before (before what?); it has a bit if a glow to it. There is a richness and fullness I hadn't noticed before. Life resonates every day and I wake to the knowledge that we are so loved. I can do nothing but love back and be a place for reflection of light in the world.

How does the hearts door open? Is it automatic? Do we simply open the door with intent and invite the flow of the Holy Spirit? I don't know. The breath enters. I am aware. Why isn't anyone talking about this? It's so <u>real</u> – but feels as if I may be on another planet. Am I just late to the party or is it part of my calling to invite and encourage others to join in?

Reality

Do you see the light?
The golden color of sun
Kissing the field, your cheek, your hair?
Do you see wings?
Strong soft feathers, lifting the fallen,
soaring to the heavens, rustling in your heart?

Do you see water?
Deep clear blue of heaven
running in rivers, pooling in lakes, falling from your eyes?

You are awake, my friend.
Open your heart,
empty it
And be filled.

Is this life I am living an illusion? I struggle with this question because my new reality seems so, well, unreal. I can see when I was (or am) living in darkness, or living without intent. I see clearly when I was not living in the light of the world. I am painfully aware when I choose not to stand in that light. Much of what I once believed to be real was merely a life of illusion; it was living in the shadow of truth. I don't know how or why it has happened, but I feel awake to God's presence. This new sight allows me to experience life in amazing abundance, reverence and awe. It allows me the freedom to experience life in greater abundance – both joy and sorrow, love and pain, grace and mercy.

Aha!

Sow for yourselves righteousness, Reap the fruit of unfailing love, And break up your unplowed ground, for it is time to seek the Lord, Until he comes and showers righteousness on you. Hosea 10:12

"Busy is the answer." Glenn's words have been echoing in my head for the last couple weeks. Huh? It contradicts what I usually hear. "Slow down", "You do too much", "Don't burn the candle at both ends." But when we talked the other day, it is his four words, "busy is the answer" that have echoed in my head.

I thought I was so smart. I thought I was a smart farmer saving some seeds to get me through tough times. I was saving some seeds for reserve. Maybe the truth is a good farmer saves some seeds, but a great farmer trusts in the Lord and sows them all. It is only then that the yield is overwhelming and beyond all dreams. God provides for us each and every day. I used to feel as if I had only so much to give. Ha! It's all God's to give. Every bit of it – and oh, what joy!

Pentecost Sunday

Blessed are those whose strength is in you, Who have set their hearts on pilgrimage. As they pass through the valley of Baca, they make it a place of springs; The autumn rains also cover it with pools. They go from strength to strength till each appears before God in Zion. Psalm 86:5-7

This morning, on Pentecost Sunday, I awoke with complete laryngitis. It was so strange that on this day, the day of the Hoy Spirit, my voice was completely gone. I love the story in Acts when the Holy Spirit is given to all people – and have often thought how cool it must have been to be a part of this large community of voices speaking together and being understood. But today for the first time, I realized the story is less about the <u>people</u> speaking and more about the Holy Spirit moving through people. So on this Day of Pentecost, I could hardly utter any words – and so, quieted, I heard.

The answer is about being busy. It IS about taking action. It is about inviting and allowing the Holy Spirit, the spirit of restlessness to stir up my calm, quiet life. I realized today that it matters less about <u>what</u> I do – and probably matters more that I do something. There are important parts, if you will, to faith growth. And there is a time for hearing, and a time for pondering, a time for being but there is most definitely a time for action. Jesus repeatedly tells us to *go!* and make disciples of all people. It is the call to action that He constantly asks for. I don't need to worry about doing the "right" thing, or making the "right" choice. This fear halts my journey.

Walking on the highway with Jesus guarantees we will never be alone and he will guide us every step of the way, moving us from strength to strength. Jesus promises that he will love us to pieces no matter what – and fall down we will. True living is not worrying about "saving" myself, or my energy or my time. It is about giving it all away. God will and does provide. So, on this Holy Day, the day of Pentecost I give great thanks for

God the Father, God the Son, the Holy Spirit and the teachers he has placed in my life. It is in great thanks and trust and hope and love and joy that I can and will say "yes."

It's another one of those crazy contradictions, like in all the parables. Is there any difference between giving and receiving, or doing what you love and loving what you do, or being and doing? In God's world, in his kingdom, they are so much the same. It's almost as if you stay doing only one of those parts for too long you don't advance. You don't mature. Maybe that's why when the rich young man asks Jesus how he can live a more full life and Jesus answers to follow the rules and the young man retorts "I have been doing that all my life" that Jesus says well, then – if that's not working for you fellow, do a 360. Because that's what living in the kingdom is all about. It is about over turning those tables. It is about turning them upside down and doing the ying instead of the yang - or maybe even better, doing them TOGETHER AT THE SAME TIME. It is then that we find ourselves in the glorious kingdom.

What shall I wear?

But when the king came in to see the guests, he noticed there was a man not wearing wedding clothes. 'Friend' he asked, 'how did you get in here without wedding clothes?' The man was speechless. "Then the king told the attendants, 'Tie him hand and foot, and throw him outside into the darkness, where there will be weeping and gnashing of teeth." "For many are invited, but few are chosen." Matthew 22: 11-14

He was invited to the wedding party. He was one of the chosen guests, but did he really get it? He responded to the wedding invitation by coming, but he refused to wear the wedding clothes. This story always seemed so confusing to me until I learned that the host of the wedding party always provided the clothes for his guests. It wasn't as if this man couldn't afford proper attire. He was invited to an all-inclusive party.

Did this man get Jesus with his heart, or did he just come to the wedding because everyone else was going? Did he just show up because he thought it was the right thing to do? Did come because he felt he should or had to? How often have I been a believer like this man, showing up but choosing not to wear the garments provided? How often have I simply gone to church, wearing a cross, going through the motions without truly engaging in Christ? How often have I showed up for this life of mine and not believed with my whole heart? This is the ultimate betrayal. God provides our party clothes for this life through the Holy Spirit. How often have I refused to wear his clothes of love, joy and compassion?

Listening

Their children, who have not known, will hear and learn to fear the Lord your God as long as you live on the land which you are about to cross the Jordan to possess. Deuteronomy 31:13

I was in the shower this morning and heard Rookie outside barking. I had asked one of the kids (really I just yelled at my son from upstairs) to let the dog in. But when I got out of the shower, he was still outside barking. Standing in the hallway, soaking wet with only my towel wrapped around me, I yelled again downstairs, calling over the railing, "Let the dog in!" I stood there dripping wet, towel askew and began the lecture of responsibility. My audience stood below, looking up at me with wide unbelieving eyes. Blah, blah, blah.

As I was talking at my son about listening, it hit me. I realized how little I listen. Really, do I listen to my children? Do I hear my friends? Most importantly, do I listen to God? We must listen. We must listen for His voice, His word, and His direction. We must listen for His whisper and then take action. I see I have missed this step. I have forgotten to teach the children to listen to GOD. I have been so busy yelling, "Listen to me!!!" I must teach them to listen. I must teach them to listen to God, to listen with their whole heart. And then I can ask them to listen to me.

Seeking

For I know the plans I have for you, declares the Lord, Plans to prosper you and not to harm you, Plans to give you a hope and a future. Then you will call upon me and come and pray to me, and I will listen to you. You will seek me with all your heart. I will be found by you, declares the Lord, and bring you back from captivity. Jeremiah 29:11-13

I have spent much of my life seeking, always looking for the right shirt, the right lot, and the right cabin property. Always looking for God. Do seekers find what they are looking for, or are seekers found because God has sought them? In all of my seeking I never found God. It was not until I stilled my noisy life that God's presence filled the deep. It was not until my heart was quieted that the waters filled up to overflowing. It was not until then that I realized God found me. I think it was my way of thinking that so often kept me from God! It was by His grace, not because I found him, but he found me- I went from a seeker to a seer. I stopped shoving stuff in the vessel of my heart. Perhaps I was trying to stop the bleeding, the pain and the loneliness. Perhaps I just bought into the "reality" this world offers. Perhaps I didn't know how to open the windows of my heart and live with fresh air and space. I didn't know how important it was to empty the vessel of my heart.

I'm not sure how I found the path. I was given a question and I asked God in. He had been right there in that very room, in every minute of every place I had ever been and I was running around like a maniac looking everywhere else. Have you ever done that with a pair of mittens or keys? Lost them and frantically searched through the house for them, only to find that they had been in your hand the whole time? Consider the magi, the wise men from the east who came to Herod and asked "Where is the one who has been born King of the Jews? We saw his star in the east have come to worship him." The magi were well-educated men, wise astronomers and well connected. They didn't just set out on their own to worship Jesus. God LED them with his light, the star. They followed the star until God brought them to the place where Jesus lay. Their wisdom rested in the fact that they followed God. They found Jesus not on their own accord, but because God found them and brought them to the baby, our King.

Julie Maijala Lundquist

Calling Me Out of the Darkness

Breath of Spirit
Blows through hair like fingers
Gently sculpting wings
Transforming humans
Into angels on earth

I was tired and crabby. I had blown the entire day without really blessing anyone. I had baked pies, cleaned the house, shopped for groceries and I wanted to lick my paw. Couldn't anyone see how exhausting this was? Couldn't anyone see that this was not the life I wanted to live, the poor stepsister Cinderella slaving away while everyone else was at the party? The mommy monster saw it's opening and crashed out.

Barking orders and yelling at my precious children, I was a rotten egg. I looked into the mirror than night while rushing out the door (to church, of all places) and what an awful creature I saw. There was no light and I was exhausted like a leftover TV dinner gone bad. We packed it up and hustled in the car to go to the Thanksgiving service (I wanted to skip, but Megan really wanted to go). I was a total Fitch. We parked, marched into the church building and dropped off yet another obligation. Of course, I had to bring "goodies", too.

After dropping off the cookies, I saw a friend, or perhaps, she saw something other than me. She saw the shell of me, inhabited by the Monster. "Where are you?" she asked. She didn't miss a beat. She didn't avoid or pamper me. She simply hugged me and she said, "You are beautiful. I love you." That was all. She called me out of the darkness, an angel of the light. What a friend. I dropped my garbage. There was room in my heart and my light was shining again. Radiant, I went to worship, ready to ask for forgiveness and give thanks.

Eagle

At that very time He cured many people of diseases and afflictions and evil spirits; And He gave sight to many who were blind.
Luke 7:21

I saw a bald eagle flying over the neighborhood. At first I thought I was seeing things, but I looked again and it was an eagle! It seemed to fly above my car as I followed it down Connelly Parkway, past the pond and over the Super America parking lot. I was so excited. I got out of my car and stood in the middle of the parking lot looking up at that beautiful creature. It circled above my head, about 20 feet up. I saw all of his beauty, the power of his beak, thick strong legs and sun reflecting off his eyes as he looked down at me. There were people all around, talking on cell phones, pumping gas, running in and out of the store, but it was as if I was alone with this amazing creature. My heart wanted to burst. The majesty, the strength, the beauty, the grace. Here it was, soaring right above me.

Look, I wanted to shout, but no one was listening. No one was looking. It was as if for those moments I was resonating alone with this beautiful creature. I don't know how long I stood there in the parking lot at Super America, but time stood still before I watched the eagle fly out of sight.

I heard a car door slam shut and someone approached me from behind, I turned and said, "Did you see it? Did you see the bald eagle?" She said she didn't see it, but said she had been watching me from her car. "I was wondering what you were looking at." We walked into the store and I bought a diet Pepsi and asked the clerk if he had seen the eagle. He said he hadn't but he was wondering what I had been looking at.

I wonder how many people saw that eagle today. I wonder how many miracles and blessings I miss because I am not looking. I wonder how much beauty I miss and will never see because I am still so blinded, because I simply forget to look.

Arrogance

"The place you are right now God circled on a lamp for you." Hafiz

I asked my children's teachers to let me be with the kids. When I volunteer I want to teach. I didn't want to be stuck in the back room working on the die cutting machine or doing other "boring" jobs. In their graciousness, they have given me freedom to be with the students.

One morning, I went in to help with book club and I found the students were away from the classroom. They were attending a school program. Instead, the teacher had left me a note asking if I would do some work she needed help with. In my opinion, it was "busy work." Stapling, coloring, hanging up stuff in the classroom, die cutting. I could feel my peacock feathers rising. What a waste of my time. I could be at home doing something productive, I could be at home doing something important. The second my thoughts hit my heart, I knew I had better change my tune.

I decided at that moment to believe in "love whatever your hands find to do." I decided to trust God that I was indeed being called to do these tasks this day. I chose to welcome this new assignment. I started with die cutting first, since I enjoyed it the least. The die cuter is back in a little office with poor lighting. Standing in between the racks of paper it feels like spending time in solitary confinement. But this day as I walked back to the office, I chose to go with a joyful heart. I began to cut and I found a rhythm to the job. I noticed the smell of the construction paper, the sharp edges of the die cutter and the squishy part of the sponge. I found myself enjoying the process. I was enjoying the job by experiencing the details with all of my senses. It was a blessing to be back there in the quiet. I found myself at peace.

Then came a great reward. A woman walking past the room happened upon me in the back corner. I must have caught her eye and she took a step backwards and asked if I was the mom of those "three darling kids." She told me she works on the playground at recess and has noticed how beautiful and kind Megan, Mick and McKenzie are. "They are just blessings", she said, "they bring so much light to the school."

Needless to say, I was speechless. Time and time again God amazes me with bounty. In my menial giving, He always showers me with riches. Planning my day isn't so much about prioritizing my tasks and deciding what job is right for "Julie the Great." It is about trusting God is present everywhere and in every task I do. It is about choosing to live in joy, no matter where I am or what I am doing.

The truth is to live in anticipation. It is to live looking right where you are, keeping your eyes on the prize. I see a life of anticipation as living in hope and faith that God's goodness is indeed pouring forth in the world now, today, this very minute and will continue to be in the future. But the other part of anticipation is trust. It is trust that God's abundance will never fail. It is trust that you need not worry about later, because your only job NOW is to stand in the presence of God. And that means being willing to be fully present in this life and realize (trust) you are exactly where you are supposed to be. Right now, wherever you are and wherever you will be is hallowed. Truth is always and unchangeable.

Coaching

Thus says the Lord, your redeemer, the Holy One of Israel, "I am the Lord your God, who teaches you to profit, who leads you in the way you should go." Isaiah 48:17

We grew up playing soccer, my sister and I. I love playing the game. I love team; I love being outside and running with others towards a common goal. Soccer is in my blood and as I got older, I realized I had learned many life lessons on the soccer field. I have been blessed with an abundance of good coaches and I wanted to give that same gift to other players, so I began to coach. Sometimes, I can't help but wonder what if God is the coach and we are the players? Am I fulfilling his expectations of being a true athlete? What are his expectations? What are mine? Am I living this life like a true athlete, competing not for the prize but for a relationship with God?

Too often, towards the last half of the season, I hear coaches ask themselves why they are devoting their precious time and resources to coaching? Parents on the sideline begin complaining about what you are not doing, who is playing or not, and fans become obsessed with the win/loss record. Players, coaches and parents become distracted from the truth of the game. We start to look at the sport instead of seeing the truth in athletics. We become consumed focusing on short-term goals, the ego, glamour, reputation and the measuring of success only by the wins and losses of our team. We do this instead of keeping our eyes on the real prize, the long-term goals of athletics. By mid season it can be easy to forget about the importance of how you play the game. We can forget to pay attention to the beauty of the athlete, the strength of the body and the sense of community that is a vital part of the season. We can lose sight of justice and respect, and our motto of "do your best" can easily sway into "be the best." We, as coaches, can avoid in many of these problems by clearly communicating our intent.

In order to do that, we must first ask ourselves some tough questions. We must spend some time reflecting on what we value. We must declare our values with players and parents. I have found it freeing to sit down with the athletes and discuss my values before the season begins. The hard part begins when we realize we must apply our values to *all* aspects of coaching. This even applies to situations on and off the field. When problems arise and you need to make decisions or deal with issues, go back to your values.

I love to coach because I love the athletes. The challenge is in meeting them where they are at – attitude, skill, and ability. When I walk onto the field for practice or a game, I need to remember why I am here. I am here to love the kids. I enjoy them, their freedom of movement and their strength and humor. It's true, try laughing – at yourself and with the kids. Play! I get so frustrated when we spend so much time coaching in the monotony of practice. It's all play – change your attitude, change your own behavior and watch them grow.

Teach the basics. Regardless of age, we must teach basics on the field. That means skill as well as character building. We must hold tight to the adage of "do your best", whether at practice, school, or during games. We must listen for the undercurrent of ego and conceitedness of "be the best" in the language that we use. We must refrain from comparisons and instead focus on the beauty of the game and the players. Don't allow players to talk about how much better they are in comparison to others. Some will point out flaws in others so they can feel better about themselves, some players are really afraid of not being liked, or not good enough. Coaches need to reassure their players that they are growing. Encourage them to talk about the greatness of your own team. In doing so, it helps all players to remember that everyone has a role on the team. No matter what that role is – if it is starting the game or sitting on the bench for the first half, all members of the team must choose to be supporting and encouraging. And in the most basic of values, we must teach personal responsibility. Each player must show up. There is no middle ground. Athletes are either 100% in or they are completely out of the game. Athletes must be responsible for communicating with the coach, for all gear, game equipment, etc. We must clearly declare our expectations.

Finally, appreciate the beauty and justice of athletics. As coaches, we must appreciate the art of an athlete. Look for grace and beauty in the rough. If you see a great play, praise it – even if it is for the other team. Look for hard work and effort. Look for passion and desire to play. Coach fairly and encourage our athletes to play fairly at all times. Don't resort to cheap play just because the referee isn't going to call it. Don't teach kick and run soccer just because you have fast enough players that can get away with that kind of play – this year. We need to think long term and continue to grow and develop our players.

We need to include character building in our coaching, integrating our values into all parts of our life. We must teach how to win with humility and lose with grace. We must teach that fair is not always equal. We must call out the good. Name the gifts that you see in each and every player. Teach your players how to build each other up, not with false, unprecedented praise, but through support and encouragement. It's been said so many times before, but teach the power of a positive attitude. It is true, if you change your mind you change your life. A true athlete competes not for the prize, but for the joy of the game, the passion that she has for simply playing.

Expectations:

All athletes must arrive at practice ready to play. That means at the designated starting time, athletes must have equipment on and be ready.

All athletes must contact the coach directly if she knows she will miss practice or games. Athletes that miss practice will not be allowed to start the next game.

All athletes will play a fair amount this season. Remember, fair doesn't mean equal – and remember that the season is longer than one game. All athletes will receive coaching and be developed according to their ability.

During games, all athletes must sit as a team and participate in the game- even while sitting on the bench. All athletes will be leaders on and off the field.

All athletes must be willing to learn and develop areas of play that may not be their "favorite." All members of the team must work together.

All athletes must work as a team. This means tucking in shirts, wearing designated uniforms, etc.

All athletes will respect the art of soccer – the game itself, the coaches, fellow athletes (including the other team), the equipment, the referees and the fans.

Sacrifice

"But go and learn what this means: 'I desire compassion and not sacrifice,' for I did not come to call the righteous but the sinners. Matthew 9:13

We must constantly offer a sacrifice of praise, do good and share with others. This is our sacrifice. It is not the sacrifice of being less than who we are created to be. It is not the sacrifice of playing small that Christ is asking for. It is simply the sacrifice of praise and the outpouring of God's amazing love towards everyone that we meet.

We hide our light by being quiet when we should speak, by denying the light, going with the crowd, not sharing our light and ignoring the needs of others. God expects our belief to penetrate into <u>all</u> areas of our lives, not just Sundays or during dinner and bedtime prayer. We must extend our heart to all people and circumstances, at all times. We cannot assume that going to church and being good is enough. We must love God with all our heart, mind, body, and soul.

Compassion

When Jesus went ashore, He saw a large crowd, and He felt compassion for them because they were like sheep without a shepherd; and he began to teach them many things. Mark 6:4

I am not sure compassion can be worked on or developed by us. That might be a bit like playing dress up and simply trying on clothes rather than experiencing a change of heart. Compassion is an action that comes from the inside out, motivated by love coming straight from the heart. It is about action, compassion is most definitely a verb.

In Mark we are told a story of the disciples and Jesus. After a long day of work, Jesus sees that his friends are tired and hungry. He sees with compassion and takes action. Jesus tells them to come with him to a quiet place in order to rest and get something to eat. But when they arrive by boat to this solitary place, hoards of people are waiting for them. There are thousands waiting for Jesus. I can't imagine what the disciples thought when they saw the shore crowded with more people - and in their quiet resting spot. I imagine some eye rolling and huge sighs of anxiety. I know after I have a busy day and head home for rest only to find chaos, I often don't look at my husband and children with compassion. But Jesus did. He looked at those masses of people and had compassion on them.

Jesus doesn't miss a beat. He hops out of that boat (probably even with a spring in his step) and begins to teach. The bible actual says, "He began to teach them MANY things." He didn't cheat and try to give them the Cliff's Notes version. He didn't skip over a few of the middle pages of the book just so he could read the last page, say goodnight, turn out the lights and go to bed. Tired and hungry he still gives much.

He teaches the crowds and he teaches his friends. The disciples are tired and hungry. As a matter of fact, if I were one of them I would also remember that it was Jesus' idea to get some food and rest. The disciples come to Jesus and tell him it is late and he should send these people away. The disciples are done giving, they want to go and get some food. But

Jesus sees them, he truly sees them and He looks on his disciples with compassion. Jesus lovingly teaches them yet another spiritual lesson. Jesus provides them with physical nourishment by telling his disciples to GIVE the people something to eat. Jesus offers himself as nourishment through instruction to his disciples. Jesus teaches them that it is in giving wholly and completely of ourselves with love for others that we are actually filled. It is somehow in this act of "going out" that the power of the Holy Spirit works to heal and fill. Jesus teaches us that by doing good, by allowing goodness and compassion to exit out in to the world we are all filled.

Compassion is all about being moved by the heart. Jesus was compassionate by bringing the disciples to a place they could learn. It is funny that Jesus brought them to a place completely opposite of where they thought they would find rest. When the disciples found it filled with noise and crowds, they grew even wearier. But Jesus showed them how to be filled by giving. Through compassion we, too, find spiritual peace and nourishment. It is being open to receive the gift and then choose to give it away that is our work. Compassion is about saying yes to God.

Compassion is love moved to action coming from the heart. People used to believe compassion came from the seat of the bowels. It was known as the movement of love and pity. What a strange place to think about compassion, but truly there is not much I can do to make my bowels work. They just work for me. If I get a little plugged up in the compassion department, the only way I know how to remedy the situation is by movement and healthy nourishment. Sounds a lot like what we are asked to do each and every day. Turn to God for our daily bread, get out there, cast some love and compassion happens.

Dear God, I give you my whole heart and my whole life this very day.
Open me to receive your abundance of blessings so your love may
overflow out of my hands, mouth, feet and heart. Lord, we believe you
and your Spirit reside in each one of our hearts. Open our eyes Lord
that we may see your face in every person we meet and humbly and
graciously respond generously because of the great love you have
given us. Lord, soften our hearts so they are tender to the touch of those

in need around us - even when we are tired and hungry. Lord, we trust in your abundance and presence and are so grateful for your teachings. It is in your great and almighty name that we pray to your son, Christ Jesus.

Bless Me

And all things you ask in prayer, believing, you will receive.
Matthew 21:22

I was at church the other day, and a child sneezed and immediately said, "Bless me!"

I need the wisdom to accept the gift of blessing. I need to be bold enough to ask for a blessing. We need to ask and be willing to receive the great blessings God has promised us. We must claim our inheritance.

Lay It Down

No one has taken it from me, but I lay it down on my own initiative. I have authority to lay it down, and I have authority to take it up again. This commandment I have received from my Father. John 10:18

When Jesus speaks of laying down our life, he speaks so much more than literally. The life he refers to, as "my life" is the life of the world, my worldly self, my ego and conceit, my pride, my fear. He tells me to put all these aside for my friends, my brothers and sisters, for all of creation.

I must get out of the way and let God work in and through me. This is the "work" that we are called to do. It is work for me to get out of the way, to let God do His thing. When we see His amazing work in our lives, we have no choice but to want to give Him thanks and praise. We must choose our work with intent – or we drift away. We must choose to know God.

Will I forget?

As for me, this is my covenant with them, Says the Lord. My spirit who is on you and my words I have put in your mouth will not depart from your mouth, or from the mouths of your children, or the mouths of their descendants, from this time on and forever, says the Lord. Isaiah 59:21

I sometimes worry I will forget what I have learned. What if I forget about the truth of living and become lost again? John tells us Jesus sent the Holy Spirit to remind us all what Jesus said and taught. Jesus promises he left us with the power of the Holy Spirit to comfort, stir and remind. What a relief. Living the Way is an education from the Father. His truth is a full ride scholarship; all we have to do is ask. We must ask for pruning, for new growth. We learn simply by listening and living.

God teaches how to live and bless others. For so long I muscled my way, trying to figure things out myself, instead of trusting that God is indeed at work. I tried to push him out of parts of my heart because I was afraid of where he would lead me. But see, when I humbly come before God and listen to the passion and desire he has placed in my heart, I can trust He will guide me and encourage me. If God can reach a successfully messed up middle class woman who pretended like she always had it together, there is no one he can't touch. God offers his free gift of grace to all people, at all times. Living a life of anticipation, hope and wonder means good adventure all the days of your life. And that's a life worth living.

Work

The Holy Spirit also testifies to us about this. First he says: This is the covenant I will make with them after that time, Says the Lord, I will put my law in their hearts, And write them on their minds. Hebrews 10:15

Not occupation or trade, but intentional choice to choose faith not fear, love not hate, humility not pride, temperance not indulgence, and justice for all instead of selfish ego. These choices, these works, are not to be done just on Sundays, at church, or only with big life choices, but within every small detail of my life. That means living in prayerful, powerful personal relationship with Christ.

It requires us to move beyond the intellectual, beyond simply thinking about, to acting on and living in the spirit of God. It is our work to commune *with all* in every aspect of our life, every path we take. Our work is to make an intentional choice not to drift away, but to step closer to God. It is about asking the Holy Spirit to continually teach and work through us and in word and open our lives. It means surrendering to God and asking Him to work in my life so that this way of living may bring Him glory and honor.

It is much easier for me to accept that Jesus died for me – than it is for me to live each and every day one day at a time. It is my work to trust God completely, everyday. I must trust God is here today and will be here tomorrow. Even more, past, present, future – I trust God was here, God is here, and God will be here tomorrow. We must pursue <u>faith</u> by mere works, we must not chase down righteousness. Instead, we must work to pursue faith through sheer trust in the Lord.

Books

But wisdom that comes from heaven is first of all pure; The peace loving, considerate, submissive, full of mercy and good fruit, impartial and sincere. James 3:17

I am so very thankful for the mentors in my life, the authors, the marvelous travels and extraordinary journeys I have taken through literature. One of my greatest joy is cracking open a new book, smelling the pages and diving in. What a wonder to find authors that spoke to my heart and feel instantly connected. But somewhere along the line I forgot to enjoy them. I stopped applying what I was reading to my life. I became obsessed with reading. I used books as an escape, as a way to avoid being fully present with what was happening in my life.

As an adult, too often I read without application and would fall into rich and lovely lives on the pages and stopped living my own. I missed out on my life in the here and now. I can only remember some vacations by what I read – not where I was, what we did or whom I was with. I missed out on the very people God had sent for me – to teach me, to love, to play with. Books have so much to teach, but if reading doesn't add to our life and only provides a means of escape, it can lead to a very lonely place. The gift of reading is found in relationship between reader and the writer. The gift is found in opening or creating space where new thoughts or insight can take root and grow. The gift an author gives to the reader is the invitation to community. As readers we are invited to become a part of something larger than ourselves. We are invited to experience life through another's eyes, to hear another's story, to learn that God is indeed active in the lives around us now, in the past, and he will be there too in the future. We must take this heart knowledge and go back out into the world to make a difference in our life and the lives around us.

Too often, reading was a way to "prove" my self worth. I felt great pride in having been so well read. I believed I couldn't come up wise or intelligent perspectives on my own. I worried they wouldn't be right. I believed I was too stupid and uninformed to have opinions of my own. I believed that to be well read was honorable. But I have learned that the truth is indeed in us. By listening and trusting, I learned that knowledge and wisdom runs much deeper that I ever imagined. It lies at the core of every heart, in every man, woman and child. We need to only learn to listen for the great teaching of truth and love. The truth is that God's wisdom is available to all.

Things Left Undone

Just as the Lord had commanded Moses his servant, so Moses commanded Joshua, and so Joshua did; He left nothing undone of all that the Lord had commanded him. Joshua 11:15

Dear Lord,
Forgive me for the things that I have done. But maybe even more wholeheartedly, forgive me for the things that I have left undone.

Forgive me for not living outside more, playing more, sitting still more, letting my body drink up sunshine more, holding hands more, catching more snowflakes on my tongue, rejoicing more, leaping more, dancing more, caring more, listening more, saying I love you more, laughing more, crying more, singing more, loving more, shining with God's radiance more, visiting grandma more.

Extreme Givers

Whoever receives one child like this in My name receives me; And whoever receives me does not receive me but Him who sent me. Mark 9:37

Extreme giving can be a sign of being a control freak. I often protected myself by being a giver – not a receiver. I figured that way I couldn't get hurt. It was away that I could attempt to be the one in control. But if I am going to ask Christ to bless me, I learned that I must let others bless me, too. That meant asking for the grace to accept and receive from God and other people in my life with a thankful heart.

I had a great massage the other day. I asked my massage therapist what is one of the favorite parts of her job. She talked of the give and take between the therapist and the patient. She enjoyed the communication/energy exchange that occurred during a massage session. She had come to this spa because she needed a change from her last position giving physical massage therapy to girls with eating disorders. She had left that field because she felt very frustrated. It seemed so one way. We talked about how women in today's culture tend to be born "givers." She found this to be true even when having a massage. The body/mind sometimes wants to resist relaxing. Sometimes we even resist what massage is offering. When she tried to give these young girls the gift of a massage, their bodies were not even physically able to receive it.

I began my session with a silent prayer asking the Lord to open my mind, body and soul to receive the gifts this therapist had to offer. I prayed for the spirit move through me and fill the massage therapist. With a very few words, there was movement of spirit. I made conscious effort to stay fully present. If I allowed my mind to just drift away, I wasn't able to override my muscles when they fought to stay tight. I noticed how important breathing is in relaxing. Bad air in, breath of the spirit out. Do massage therapists offer prayers up for people getting the massage? Have you ever thought about praying for your hairdresser, massage therapist or doctor?

Healing

For the heart of this people has become dull, With their ears they scarcely hear, And they have closed their eyes, Otherwise they would see with their eyes, Hear with their ears, And understand with their heart and return, And I would heal them.
Matthew 13:15

Following my ACL surgery, I was afraid to touch my wound. I wanted my knee to heal, so I kept it clean, but I really didn't touch it because I was afraid it might hurt. I remember the first day of physical therapy an amazingly beautiful nurse called me into the exam room and removed the wraps around my knee. I was apprehensive as she unwound the dressing and then took off the band-aids. I winced in anticipation; afraid she might really hurt me, even if by accident. As she placed her hands directly on my wounds tears began to roll down my face. At that moment I knew everything was good and my knee was healed. I read somewhere that our body remembers its wounds and pain even when physical hurts are not present. I believe that her simple loving touch healed my body's memories of hurt from surgery.

In that one moment, I saw how many times in my life I had moved on from pain and hurt without first healing. I realized I had warehoused them only to surface again in the future at the most unlikely times. I could see how many times my body and spirit remembered pain and hurts I hadn't let go - until I allowed myself to be healed by grace. God is the ultimate healer and continues to restore his creation, even to this day. He wants to heal us and invites us to be children of God he created us to be. He wants to place his hands on our wounded hearts and heal us. How often do we wince and pull back, too afraid that the healing might hurt?

Sometimes, I feel as if I have spent such a big chunk of my life screwing up. I surely have played a part in messing up God's amazing creation. I have refused his goodness intentionally (so often I thought it might hurt, like that day following my knee surgery); I have drifted away without even realizing how far away from home I had gone. But God, thank you God, meets us where we are. He truly accepts us as we are. He found me – and by his grace he healed me. I became awake, aware of true living- first crawling, then walking and now, thankfully, running for home.

Big Bird Alarm Clock

Our work is to wind our clock. When we were kids, my sister had a Big Bird Alarm clock. It was something we loved and it marked off all our days, elementary through high school. Kari would set it every night, and every morning Big Birds voice called to me through the wall:

Good morning, it's me, Big Bird
Don't roll over and go back to sleep.
One foot out of bed, now the other one.
O.K. Have a good day,
And don't forget to wind the clock!

I think if God made an alarm clock, he would have it say much the same thing. Good morning! It's me, God. Don't go back asleep; turn and walk with me in all that you do with intent. Choose to live. It's simple – one step, one day at a time. You've got to move – don't just lie there. O.K. You are awake. Now look for the good, name it, and greet it. Have a good day. And don't forget to give thanks and praise to God.

I Am A Sheep

Trust in the Lord and do good; dwell in the land and enjoy safe pasture. Delight yourself in the Lord and he will give you the desires of your heart. Psalm 37:3

I am a sheep. Too often I think that I must be the shepherd watching over my own flock – taking care of my children and husband, family, friends and neighbors. I need to remember that first I am a sheep. I must make sure to allow myself access to green pastures and lie besides fresh water in order to sooth my soul. I must allow myself nourishment and care. God will rescue, but we need to choose to take refuge – to live in Christ.

It is only in wholeness I can go out and build true community. It is only rested that I can then go forth and live with love and compassion, peace and joy. Wholeness is knowing the truth for my soul and for my Julie – both the light and the dark. It is knowing my strengths and my weaknesses. It is choosing to dwell in the light and stepping around the dark places when I have a choice.

God tells us to dwell, to really LIVE in the land. He isn't asking us to just show up and hang out. He hasn't sent us here on earth to live like we are just part of the "bedroom community", spending time in our residences so we could work Monday through Friday before we punch out the time clock for the weekend to really live. Every day is real. Every day is a treasure. Life is about living not acquiring, emptying not accumulating, waking not walking dead, not always pushing for more but simply LIVING IN THE LAND and going forth with great joy and praise.

Dappled Light

He said to them, "Do you bring a lamp to put it under a bowl or a bed? Instead, don't you put it on its stand? For whatever is hidden is meant to be disclosed, And whatever is concealed is meant to be brought out into the open. If anyone has ears, let him hear."
Mark 4:21-23

The high noonday sun coupled with big shade trees can be a photographer's nightmare. It is tough to get the lighting right. There are too many shadows, too many hot spots. But dappled light is truth. Maybe that is why it is so difficult to capture on film. We can photograph on a cloudy, overcast day easily enough. Even a glorious sunny morning photographs easier than dappled light (but even beautiful mornings have shadows, as well as stormy days light). But those tranquil rich abundant dappled days of summer are the most difficult to capture. Either the images are too washed out or are simply too dark. We must share both our struggles and our joys in order to build true community. To tell the story of truth we must know both our light and our dark.

Traveling Husbands

For this reason a man will leave his father and mother and be united with his wife, and the two will become one flesh.
Ephesians 5:31

I used to hit a pothole every time Paul traveled out of town on business. I wasn't used to living with a person who traveled. I grew up with my Dad home every night for dinner at the family table by 5:30pm. I don't know where I got the notion, but a part of me felt very abandoned when Paul traveled on business. I felt he was choosing work over his family – which was not the case at all – but I would dam up and close off the door to my heart while he was gone. I avoided his phone calls, pouted and sealed because I was afraid I would be hurt. I was afraid of being all alone. Part of me was mad that he got to "waltz in and out." How unfair I was to my husband. I realized I needed to give it up. I needed to see things clearly.

I opened my eyes and I saw how much Paul really cared for us. I saw how hard he worked to support our growing family. I saw that it was me that needed to change. I needed to tear down the dam that I had grown exhausted holding up. I made a conscious choice to change my tune. I expected to swept away by a raging current of sadness and despair, I had been afraid to let go of this anger towards my husband. I imagined a huge wave would come and take me under, sweeping me out in into the dark depths. I was afraid of opening the door to my heart and leaving it that way. I was afraid of being vulnerable with Paul gone.

I decided to drop my guard. I opened my door and braced myself for mighty waves of sorrow that would certainly sweep upon the shore. As I stood in the room of my heart with its doors wide open, I was shocked to find just a mere trickle of sadness. I saw how foolish I had been thinking I had to be strong and not give in, believing that I could actually control the situation by denying it. I learned that I was really just sad because I missed him while he was away. I learned that he missed us, too. When I stopped believing I NEEDED to be in control of everything, when I stopped fighting because I was afraid, the healing and the love and the abundance of light was amazing.

Paul still travels and I still miss him very much when he is gone. But now we honor the time we are together as a family and give great thanks and praise. We are learning to see the great opportunities for goodness that his travel affords all of us. We are thankful for casual dinners, early bedtimes, sleepovers in Momma's room and are learning about the gift of being able to be together without having to be physically present. The kids and I have learned how to welcome the transition and are so thankful for the opportunities we have everywhere in our life – even on the days and evenings Paul is traveling.

Bedtime Prayers

Now I lay me down to sleep,
I pray the Lord my soul to keep
If I die before I wake
I pray the lord my soul to take.

I believe this prayer may have saved my life. Ever since I was a child, my Mom and Dad prayed this nightly bedtime prayer along with "God Bless" followed by a litany of loved ones with my sister and me. I cry with joy when I realize that even while sleeping (spiritually sleeping, not being awake to knowing) God has been keeping, protecting and being faithful to my soul. This prayer fortifies my belief that the Lord indeed loves ALL his people. He loves ALL children and takes them, keeps them and meets them wherever they are on their walk. God never stops loving.

I must choose to lay "me" down. I must lay down my ego, pride and baggage and ask God to awaken his right spirit within me. In this prayer, me is my ego. My soul is Julie and includes my uniqueness, God given gifts, talents, inheritance, and my special child of God. By dying unto myself, by simply listening to God, he provides the highway that leads to living.

Parenting

While they were there, the time came for the baby to be born, and she gave birth to her firstborn, a son. She wrapped him in cloths and placed him in a manger, because there was no room for them in the inn. Luke 2:6

Oh, how I want to protect my children and keep them from avoiding mistakes I have made. When I look to the bible for parenting tips, I see that even with his only begotten son God did not stop him from experiencing pain. His mother did not keep him in a padded box afraid he might get hurt. Instead, Mary freed Jesus to do what he was called to do. She freed him and encouraged him to be whole, to believe in God. She taught him her faith, she taught him to live by heart and have the courage to experience both the pain and joy of what was to come.

Without suffering pain ourselves, we may never know the glory of life. We may never really know deep in our heart that through it all, God never leaves his children. I am certain God's heart was breaking as he watched his son dying for all mankind. I can't imagine Mary watching her beautiful baby boy crucified on the cross. Their stories set a radically different model for parenting.

Mary didn't say, "Jesus those other kids aren't playing nicely with you. Why don't you find some new friends? Jesus, they don't trust you, why don't you move on? Jesus, don't be so vulnerable, you will get your heart broken. Jesus, what do you mean you are afraid? This is nothing to be afraid of. Don't be a baby. Jesus, give me a break, don't you realize that you are 30 years old? When are you going to stand up for yourself and do something? Jesus, you are not perfect. Jesus, who in the world do you think you are?"

Instead, Jesus was loved by his Mother and Father, over and over and over again. He was taught to love instead of fear, accept instead of expect, praise instead of criticize, live open with vulnerability instead of closing off, to give instead of take, to see abundance instead of depravity and to choose refuge vs. a one time rescue. In our culture, we focus so much on expectations. " Have high expectations for your children or they will never amount to anything." But no matter what I read, the truth is more about accepting and meeting people where they are at, even our children. We must bless them and encourage them. We must trust them, love them, and know them. We must let them.

Anytime I lay my expectations on anyone else, especially my own children, I either limit or imprison them. The only place for expectation is at the feet of Christ. There I can lay anything down and expect (trust, know, believe) that I am loved and will never be alone to all the ends of the earth. How often I have placed handcuffs on those that I love, my dear husband, children and even myself– never allowing those I love to be free to grow into the child God intended. If I remove my expectations, it frees us all. I must never except of anyone what only God can deliver. I must quit expecting of my husband, children and friends only what GOD can give me.

If I expect my children to 'do better" than I have done, to go to college, to play the piano for a minimum of three years, to get good grades – then they may attain only that. They may never move beyond the limited view, the small dreams that I have. But if I accept them for who they are and trust in the greatness of God, if I trust that God can and WILL move in their lives as he has done in mine, how much more freeing is that? They will live whole and complete, unique to the life God called them to.

PAIN

For whoever wants to save his life will lose it, but whoever loses his life for me will find it. Matthew 16:25

There is nothing that we can do better or more to protect our children from feeling pain. Perhaps pain is universal. Maybe it is something we all share, something that can tear us apart or unite us. Maybe it is even something that can help build true community. I think about the uniqueness of our creation. God created us to heal. God created trees to seal, or at least that is the way it is supposed to work. Too often it seems to be the complete opposite.

Is pain felt from a sliver any different from pain inflicted by the loss of a finger? When we get past comparing whose pain is greater, or judging some pain like that from a sliver as not worthy of expressing, we must see both are experiencing hurt. Aren't both examples pain, perhaps in differing degrees, but pain nonetheless? I used to experience shards of pain and bits of heaven. Now I experience shards of pain and thundering showers of joy.

Play

Sing to him a new song; Play skillfully with a shout of joy. Psalm 33:3

Jesus played. He told stories. He was vulnerable and free, not self-conscious. He lived by heart with all of his senses employed. He was joyful and his short life reflected much movement.

Why does our culture demand no free play??? Today we even believe that to exercise, to move our bodies, we must have a club membership – or follow a program. Even art is marketed as a kit activity, as a program to follow with simple instructions and expectations as to what your creation should look like. We buy kits, programs and memberships with details outlining how to make it look right. We buy step-by-step booklets to identify what we are missing in our already fragmented lives. We spend our money attempting to fulfill limited expectations. Are we allowing ourselves to really live or are we buying into the notion that life is something that can be acquired by merely following the rules of the world?

This way of living, simply following prescribed rituals and instructions, robs us from living life to the fullest. It robs us from creating the life God intended uniquely for each of us. By not following the deepest desires of our heart, by not playing, we toss aside God's desires and hopes for each of his creation. We ignorantly settle and pluck a cheap prize from the wishing well after we have cleaned our plates instead first allowing ourselves to listen to what we really hunger for.

Abundance

People went out to him from Jerusalem and all Judea and the whole region of the Jordan. Confessing their sins, they were baptized by him in the Jordan River. Matthew 3:5-6

John the Baptist was the first guy on the block to begin baptizing. He had no competition until Jesus came along. The Pharisees sidle up to John and inform him he has some baptism competition. The Pharisees try to get him all riled up and tattle to John that Jesus is baptizing too. But John the Baptist doesn't take the bait. He says a man can receive only what is given him from heaven. He knows it is his job to prepare the way for the Lord. John's heart is filled with joy just to hear Jesus' voice. He is filled with joy to recognize his words. His heart is empty of ego, pride and competition. He is filled with joy, truly complete. John believes and trusts in the great abundance of God.

I think that the whole story of the John the Baptist and Jesus both baptizing is really about abundance. It is not about John baptizing OR Jesus baptizing. It is about John listening to his calling and Jesus listening to his. Too often I choose to see life as OR…this OR that or as BUT…but living this way is not living at all. I think God clearly (he is the three in one) is about AND, He is about abundance in truth and love. We must hold on to truth, the real world, God's world, is full of AND. When we rely on God it is all about YES! You can do both this and that. John could baptize and follow Jesus, and do it brilliantly by simply allowing God to work through his life. When we don't get in the way, miracles happen in the world of God's amazing abundance.

Service

Command them to do good, to be rich in good deeds, and to be generous and willing to share. 1 Timothy 6:18

In one of the Old Testament Bible stories, David and his army are in enemy territory. David announces he is thirsty and he would love to drink the water from a well at the Gate of Bethlehem. Three of his men break through enemy lines, draw water and carry it back for David. Can you imagine how excited they were to present him, their King, with the special water he requested? Can you imagine how proud and accomplished they might have felt? But David does a shocking thing. These men risked their lives for him to get him this water and David refuses to drink. Right there in front of them, David pours it out on the ground. Talk about regifting!

I can't imagine their reaction as David takes the precious water they risked their lives for and pours it on the ground. These three men were loyal listeners, brave, courageous and devoted servants. Men with these characteristics know God and honor him by serving others. This is why they are called mighty, not because they were fierce fighters, but because they are mighty servants. Their might is proven greater by the absence of their response to David's action. Their lack of response shows great strength. David humbles himself and pours out the water as an offering before God. He suddenly realizes the precious gift he has been given and refuses to drink water that risked the blood of his men. He knew only God is worthy of such devotion. He, too, sacrificed for God by pouring out the water and giving thanks even while in great thirst.

The mighty men are proven great by the absence of their response to David's action. What do you think the men did when they saw David pour out the water? Why isn't their reaction part of the story? Why didn't they say "We risked our lives for you so you could have some lousy water from the well where the enemy is camped out, and all you do to thank us is to pour it out?" I have said that before. They didn't say it because they knew their work, no matter what is was, was to serve God with all their might.

They gave freely because it was all for God's glory. They gave wholly and compassionately because their commander, their brother, thirsted for a drink from the eternal spring. They were devoted men courageous enough to take action, and knew how to listen to their own hearts.

If David had been focused on what the three were doing he might have risked NOT sacrificing the water they brought for him to the Lord. He might have felt he had to drink it so he wouldn't disappoint them. This story is one of might because of the abundance of servants, none of the men had ego get in the way and insisted they had to be the one who served, or who was served. We honor those who serve us by serving others. We honor God by serving others; we bring God's glory here to earth by sowing the seeds of goodness, by being fully alive to our hearts content.

Doing

He chose David his servant and took him from the sheep pens; from tending the sheep he brought him to be the shepherd of his people Jacob, Of Israel his inheritance. And David led them with integrity of heart; With skillful hands he led them. Psalm 78:70-72

In the last part of Samuel, David decides to see how well he does on his own. Instead of putting his confidence in the Lord, he counts up all his guys. He wants to see if he has an army strong enough to beat the enemies. He wants physical proof he can take the bad guys on. David calls for a census to help him count his success as a commander in chief. He puts faith in numbers instead of trusting the Lord will deliver him from all evil. After he makes the count, David grieves because he realizes he made a mistake. I love how David so often makes mistakes, and then so quickly asks for forgiveness. God does forgive.

Sight

Taking the blind man by the hand, He brought him out of the village; And after spitting on his eyes and laying his hands on him, He asked, "do you see anything?" Mark 8:23

Have you ever been able NOT to see the blessings in your life? So often I haven't seen the blessings that are right in front of my eyes – especially when they are greater than I could ever imagine. Our humanness can blind us to God's presence and the blessings he sends our way every day. We must pull the skins off that cover our eyes and be open to the presence of God's blessings in our everyday life. We must be courageous enough to ask for sight to live the amazing freedom God has for each one of us.

We must choose to focus on the blessings of each day instead of focusing on ourselves. Look at the blessings you have been given this very day. Stop for one moment and think about them. Wait a minute longer and listen to what rises from the depths of your heart. Sometimes we can see the basic ones pretty easy – shelter, food, and family. Can you see more?

God has much greater plans in store for our lives than we can ever imagine. Think about Peter (in Mark) and Jesus telling him "Get behind me Satan." Satan is whatever blinds us the presence and the glory and the blessings of God. We must trust God does indeed have a plan for each and every one of us. We must trust God will reveal his plan for us at the right time. Until then we must patiently look for the blessings he sends to us every moment of every day.

Details

Then Shadrach, Meshach and Abed-nego came out of the midst of the fire. The satraps, the prefects, the governors and the king's high officials saw in regard to these men that the fire had no effect on the bodies of these men, nor was the hair of their head singed, nor were their trousers damaged, nor had the smell of fire even come upon them. Daniel 3:27

There is an amazing story in Daniel about Shadrach, Meschach and Abednego. It is a story of God saving them from the firey furnace. It is a story of God's great protection and loving of his people. The synopsis of this story is powerful, but not to be overlooked are the details of the story. When these guys came out of the hot burning furnace alive, not a hair on their heads was singed, their pants were not burned and they didn't even smell like smoke.

I am beginning to see how much God is in the details. God didn't pull three charred burnt men from the fire. He paid attention to every detail in saving them. He paid attention their life, each hair on their head and the smell of their cloaks. If we are to be true followers of the Lord then we must pay attention to the details. It's about loving what you do. It's about welcoming the smell and warmth of clean laundry as we fold it as it comes out of the dryer. It is about noticing the crispness and color of the carrot as we cut them for dinner. It is about looking out our window and watching the nut hatch bounce up and down the tree trunk.

Mother Theresa says, "We can't do great things on earth; we can only do things with great love." It's where miracles happen. It's when God's abundance reigns down on us. It's when the gates of heaven open as we stand in the doorway welcoming our children home from school. It's when we walk out from the fiery pit, not even smelling like smoke.

Daily Living

So all the work on the tabernacle, the Tent of Meeting, was completed. The Israelites did everything just as the Lord commanded Moses. Then they brought the tabernacle to Moses,: the tent and all its furnishings, its clasps, frames, crossbars, posts and bases; the covering of ram skins dyed red, the covering of hides of sea cows and the shielding curtain; ... Exodus 39: 32-35

My sister moved. Three days ago the moving truck came and she and her family packed up and left. My whole life feels emptier. Our culture seems to focus so much on the big stuff – birthdays, Christmas, holidays - but the wonderful blessing of living close to my sister (we lived a mere 300 yards apart) taught me the little stuff is just as important. Perhaps, the little stuff is even more important. It is the day-to-day stuff I miss the most. Her simple wave from the mailbox, watching her water her plants and tend her garden, seeing the kids run over, walking past her house knowing she was getting tucked in for the night when her lights were on in her upstairs window. I miss stopping by her house and going for a morning walk. It is the little things like these that I grieve the most.

My grief is so very real and I have been taken by surprise by its intensity. I do realize my grief often honors how terrific it was living so close. Grief honors the goodness we had living as neighbors. And it is my grief, my pain, that exposes how important the small details, the nitty gritty of life is important to our living, to our loving and to our faith.

Our faith walk is *more* than church on Sunday, baptism celebrations, confirmation, Christmas service and Easter lilies. It is about being in community, it is about walking beside calm waters, looking for and seeing His beauty every day. It is about living each and every day to its' fullest. It is about welcoming change and growth, even as painful as it sometimes is. Living is about being fully present with God every day.

Grief is so much a part of life. The true definition of joy is so different from 'happy' as we know it in our culture. Joy, in the truest meaning of the word, holds the paradox of both the crucifixion and the resurrection, of both the pain of losing a loved one and the peace of knowing they are in a better place, of the pain and grief in knowing that we all make mistakes but our God is so amazingly huge that we are completely forgiven, picked back up and asked to live again and again. Maybe sometimes grief exposes the truth of living, with God even pain becomes an opportunity for growth and new life.

Amazing Beauty

But lay up for yourselves treasures in heaven, where neither moth
nor rust destroys and where thieves do not break in and steal.
Matthew 6:20

God reveals so many glimpses of astounding beauty – not only
visible, but Sprit filled awe- in my heart. I wonder if they are glimpses of
heaven. Is heaven less about a physical location and more about moment?
Is a glimpse of heaven caught in the moments we lose our limited
humanness and become spirit filled? Is a sliver of heaven experienced
when we *know* the absolute marvel of Gods abundant love and peace and
joy – even if only for a breath? I am so very thankful for spirit filled
moments that offer fragmented glimpses of the amazing abundance of
God's love for his people.

Fear

When God gives any man wealth or possessions, and enables him to enjoy them, to accept his lot and be happy with his work – this is a gift from God. He seldom reflects on the days of his life, because God keeps him occupied with gladness of heart. Ecclesiastes 5:19

I love that God promises to keep us occupied with gladness of heart. What a beautiful peaceful gift – and how many times have I not accepted it? How many times did I see God coming, gift in hand and pretty much say "No thanks, I don't need anything right now. I am doing just fine." I have done that so many times in my life before.

I remember when I was a new bride I didn't want my husband to hold the door open for me – or when we were hiking if he turned around to offer me a hand I wouldn't hold mine out to receive his help. I figured I could do things on my own, so I didn't want to waste a precious commodity of accepting help when I didn't need it. Maybe somewhere in my heart I thought love was limited and I didn't want to use it up on things I could definitely do myself.

So often fear (my belief in scarcity of love, of blessings) has clogged the abundance trying to get in my life. I know fear can turn away love – I have seen how those so afraid of losing often turn away the people that love them without ever realizing they are doing it. I see that if I am unwilling to believe in the abundance, or chose to believe I can't afford (time, money, energy) what I really want to do, I turn away God's blessing in my life. I can turn away God's amazing blessing simply by not trusting, not trying, not believing it to be true. If we operate our lives in the scarcity mode, we miss out on so many blessings.

God has promised to bless his people – every one of us. So much of my thinking was fear based. I was always thinking, planning, scheming about everything. I couldn't stop the noise. I couldn't stop thoughts from constantly bombarding me. My thoughts weren't horrible, but they were so all consuming I couldn't find any peace. I would find myself rehearsing conversations, planning what I was going to say without first listening to what other people had to offer. I carried my Franklin planner around like it was some priceless idol to worship. I fretted about everything. All these thoughts flew around inside my head and in my heart; their whirling took me out of the present tense. *Now* is the only time we find God, we find peace, joy.

Sometimes I worried about my dad's cancer so much, grieved so dearly for my sister for too long without giving it up to God. I think all this worry and grief stopped the blessings. It didn't stop God's blessing from coming (he promises he will never leave us) but my fear stopped me from receiving them. It was my constant fear and worry that barricaded the light from coming into my soul. I had to learn to stop. We obey what we worship and I spent far too long worshipping worry and fear. I spent too many sleepless nights worrying, scheming, or coming up with a plan to fix things. Stop. Choose love.

Planning

But if serving the Lord seems undesirable to you, then choose for yourselves this day whom you will serve, whether the gods your forefathers served beyond the river, or the god of the Amorites, in whose land you are living. But as for me and my household, we will serve the Lord. Joshua 24:15

I worked for years as a pharmaceutical sales representative for a fortune 500 company. We attended training classes, seminars and conferences focusing on planning and time management. We were taught the importance of prioritizing, organizing and action plans. I worshiped my Franklin Planner, spent Sunday nights prioritizing my tasks for the week and had a coronary every time I couldn't find my planner. Plain and simple, I was following another god.

When I went to many time management seminars, they brought out a big glass jar representing each week of our life. Put the important things in first, they said. I thought about my priorities – I had to pick up the dry cleaning on Monday, make it to my early morning cluster meeting and get the kids to day care – all by 8:00. Every time I tried to prioritize tasks that lay ahead of me, I put them all in the wrong places. How was I to know what was more important? So, I just winged it and tried to do everything – but was never fully doing anything.

David planned on building a beautiful temple for the Ark of the Covenant to praise God. He worked so hard to do this. But God said no, you can't build me a temple. I live in a tent. The most beautiful, well-orchestrated plans sometimes are not even minute replicas of the big dreams God has planned for us. Esther, on the other hand, had no fancy plans but finds herself a part of the Kings harem, not ever quite believing that this is where she needs to be. The story doesn't portray her as scheming and planning to get ahead. Instead, we learn Esther listens and chooses with intent to engage. She turns to God for direction as the plan unfolds. She is willing to listen and to take action each step of the way.

Like Esther's story, sometimes we will see the whole thing come together to fruition, but sometimes we don't.

When we go about our life, we must trust and believe that God is working wonders and miracles right where we are. We must prayerfully come before God and ask him to guide and direct our days. Yes, we still need to stay on track and organized, but first we need to turn to God and ask HIM to fill the large empty vessel of our life. It is only then that we realize God provides opportunities for good in all things, at all times. I am learning to check in with God and let him know what I have on my plate that day. I want him to know the commitments I have made and want to honor – and I ask God to work through me in each of these. I also let him know that I am available to be either his light or the mirror that reflects it. I ask him to fill my heart, soul and body with his spirit.

Many of my days are filled with vast depth. I listen to my heart and things that I need to get done, do. Even more often amazing things happen that I never even saw coming on my radar screen. At the end of the day, it is usually all the other stuff that fell into the cracks of my day that were richest of all. God works so often in the details of our life. If we stuff our days full of *our* priorities with no room for anyone else (God included) we are not living. God's wonders need time to unfold. Even the world was created over seven days. When I listen to the story of creation, I don't see God checking off a list, I see God being.

Big Trouble

Jesus promised those who would follow him only three things. They would be amusedly happy, entirely fearless and always in trouble.
-Greg Levoy

It is the third phrase," always in trouble", that has caught me so often in my life. I would never choose to be in trouble. I always wanted to stay OUT of trouble – even if meant going against something that I didn't really want or believe in. I wanted to be a good girl.

I am thankful to God for the courage he has given me to get in trouble. He has given me courage to speak out for the poor and oppressed – even if my views are in opposition to my family and friends. He has given me the courage to stand out against racism and class – even if I speak out in opposition of loved ones. It has gotten me in trouble with people I love dearly. I have had to choose to follow the light and speak out against vile and racist hatred. It was one of the scariest things that I have ever done – spoken out so boldly, knowing that I was indeed going to cause trouble and hurt. But I am so thankful for my new boldness. It was news to me to find such peace while getting into trouble.

Hopelessness

The Lord, the Lord Almighty, called you on that day to weep and to wail, to tear out your hair and put on sack cloth. But see, there is joy and revelry, slaughtering of cattle and killings of sheep, eating of meat and drinking of wine! "Let us eat and drink." You say, "for tomorrow we will die!" Isaiah 22:10-12

I always thought I was a person of hope. I mean, I believed in God, I believed in Jesus. I went to church. I prayed. But I had no idea I was living a life that was shot through with hopelessness. There were many parts of my life I didn't turn to God to for help. There were parts of my life I had screwed up badly by making poor choices – and I felt too responsible to ask anyone for help. Even God. I tried trusting everything and everyone except God.

I wonder if our American culture has created such excess of wealth and power that we have put our trust in everything beside God. Perhaps this worship of material things, money, time and success, has left many of us alone and in despair. Perhaps our hopelessness shows up in maxed out credit cards, high debt and closets filled with more than we can ever use, overweight bodies, or bodies starved or over ripped with muscle. There are two common responses to hopelessness – self indulgence and despair. I see too often many of my bad habits were created out of sheer hopelessness.

I grew up in a hard working family that often struggled to make ends meet. I knew the power and influence money could have on a family. So, somewhere in my heart I had chosen to act as if money didn't matter, as if it was something I wanted no part of. Because I never saw money as a blessing, I never honored it. I never honored the fact that our jobs, our bank accounts, our finances, our possessions were blessings that too, needed to be honored by giving God thanks and praise. They needed to be honored with respect. I never respected money.

In the Old Testament the people of Israel knew the end was coming. They knew their city was surrounded by enemies and there was no way out. Instead of repenting, instead of turning to God for help, the people of Jerusalem partied and feasted. They killed their choice animals for lavish parties. They drank the first fruits of wine, toasting one another "No more worries, tomorrow we die!" They used every means possible to avoid turning to God. They fortified cities, moved water supplies, built walls. They trusted in everything and everyone except God and they knew it wasn't working. As their enemies closed in on them from all sides, God's people never turned to him. They never asked for forgiveness.

Is this any different than today? Did I spend because of despair and hopelessness?? Did I follow advice from financial advisors on the Today Show and Suzie Orman before I ever considered talking to God about my worries? Did I spend because I stopped trusting God would provide, because I thought that I needed to buy something *real* to fill the void? Was I reckless because part of me no longer believed God cared? Did I try everything in my power to piss away even this gift God was trying to give me? Was I living my days any differently than the people of Jerusalem a thousand years ago?

Shopping

So god created man in his own image; in the image of God He created Him; male and female he created them.Genesis 1:27

While shopping at the Mall of America the other day, 2 college girls stopped me and said, "You are absolutely gorgeous." How come I want to believe it was a joke? How come I wrestle with myself for not believing their words? I heard their voices and listened hard for the punch line. I glanced behind me for the group of people watching, waiting, and laughing. I saw no one. Forgive me for my unbelief.

Painting or Billboard?

We can make our minds
So like still water
That beings gather about us
That they may see, it may be,
Their own images, and
So live for a moment with a clearer
Perhaps even a fiercer life
Because of our quiet.
-William Butler Yeats

I had my 20th year class reunion. I was uncomfortable with the question "so, what do you do?" and even more frustrated by my answer. I struggled with my need to conform to a "job title", the need for my ego to be filled with a printable business card version the says Julie = success. I was uncomfortable with running off my mouth and saying nothing. I was uncomfortable because I didn't have much to say.

Hindsight is always 20/20 but what if you asked me today, what would I say? I am a wife, a mom, a daughter, a sister, and a friend following a faithful calling. I would simply share a few details of my life with great care. I want to offer a painting to a world that asks for a billboard. My job, my purpose, is to wake each day and to praise God for my world and my life – and ask that he reveal himself to me everywhere I go and in every person I meet. Christ doesn't handout business cards – he gives us calling cards that don't take us out of the world, but send us into it.

Focus

Therefore I say to you, whatever things you ask when you pray, believe that you receive them, and you will have them. Mark 11:24

God tells us to ask for what we want. Prayerfully get quiet, listen and name your vision or goal. At that very minute we need to believe and trust that God is working to make that possible. The amazing beauty of God's world is that his gifts are not only given at the outcome, but every step along the way. It is about trusting and checking in with God every day knowing that by following God, He helps us find the straightest path. It is our work to believe this even when we can't see how the tasks of the day are related to our goal or request.

I think about things that I have prayed for - and most of my prayers have been answered. Not always on my timetable, not always exactly how I thought things would be, but more often than not they have come to fruition far better than I have ever dreamed. I must trust when I pray that God will indeed fulfill my prayer soon, that God is working on fulfilling my prayer and it will take a little time, or that God won't fulfill my prayer because He has something far greater in mind. It all goes back to trust. I must trust God enough and believe that he always has my best interest in mind.

Julie Maijala Lundquist

Hope

Hope is to leave a better world for our children.
Hope is to pass on a blessing to future generations.
Hope is to leave good soil.

I attended a meeting to review the landscape design plans for a new office that was being built. It was a good basic plan, but the designers placed three Burr Oak trees within 10 feet of the office building. Burr Oaks are traditionally very large trees. The design placed three of these oak trees within a 40 x 12 space next to a large new office building. I asked if the tree was the right choice for that place. The landscape designer laughed and said that it wouldn't be a problem in my lifetime.

My heart was saddened. When are we going to realize we create problems today by NOT paying attention to tomorrow? When are we going to realize how many opportunities we miss out on making a difference because we don't care about anything unless it impacts my life right now? Broken? Throw it away and buy a new one. Feeling empty? Fill up with food, shopping bags or gossip about what a loser your neighbor's kid is. No need to think about tomorrow - just get the biggest bang for your buck.

Who cares about the environment? Our abuse of God's creation won't matter much in our lifetime. Let's fill those garbage dumps with even more packaging. Let's allow industry to pollute the skies and water because to change to more environmentally ways may be too costly. Today, who cares about planting a beautiful Burr Oak tree 12 feet from the building, where it will certainly experience stress and disease because of poor growth space and soil conditions and wreak havoc on the building structure for years to come?

What does it matter? It won't make a difference in my lifetime. But what of our children? What of the next generation? Sarah Groves sings "Remind me of this in every decision, I reap what I sow. I can pass on a curse or a blessing, for those I don't even know." I was surprised the landscape designer actually said it out loud and people laughed. I saw how many times the choices I have made in my own life had laughed in the face of God's creation.

Peace maker VS. Peace Keeper

Blessed are the peacemakers, for they shall be called sons of God.
Matthew 5:9

For many years I have prided myself on my great ability to peace keep. At home, I felt responsible for keeping and maintaining harmony (at almost any cost). When I worked in corporate, I was brought into dysfunctional groups to help bring about harmony and resolution.

The truth is being at peace does not mean being of one mind or opinion. Peace does not equal same. When I asked our children if they knew any peacemakers, the first person that they mentioned was Martin Luther King Jr. He certainly expressed his beliefs – and they were radically different than the majority of people. But he believed in true peace, the love of Christ and the love of our neighbors as ourselves.

We make peace by forgiving ourselves and our neighbors. We make peace by listening to our neighbor's joys and struggles – and hearing with compassion. We make peace by honoring each other's differences and loving each other just the same.

I have come to realize that my peacekeeping was prideful. My desire to keep the peace stemmed from the fact that I was truly most concerned with me not being the one in trouble or the one who was wrong. Peace making had less to do with faith and more to do with in my own ego and control. I believed, somehow, that if there was conflict, I was responsible to fix it. Which really meant that I thought that I was the ONLY one capable of fixing it. This Peace Keeping put way too much stress on me in the form of worry and fretting. My peacekeeping lacked peace.

The Peace of Christ differs from worldly peace. Worldly peace tells us we must all be alike. We must conform to the beliefs, the dress, and the language of the dominant. True peace comes from the unity of God. It is only from the unity between all creatures great and small. Peace is about different people, unique lives, and many languages all coming together to make a change in the world. Peace is about bringing glory to God. Peace is about following your own map. To hide in the sand, to be afraid of conflict, or to be afraid of speaking your own heart is to live imprisoned. It is only in living in Gods will that we are truly free and at peace.

Thank God

We deserve nothing. All is Gods. Luke 12:7

Last night when we got home from the hospital, McKenzie found yet more gifts awaiting her, piles of them sat on the front doorstep. I couldn't help but grow anxious. Here was my healed, healthy beautiful girl being lavished (once again) with so many gifts. I have to be honest, there was a big part of me that wanted to say "let's return these gifts or give them away to children back at the hospital who are really sick" (read here DESERVE them). As if I/ you/me/my daughter ever DESERVE the gifts we are given.

When we receive a gift, Jesus teaches us that our response is THANKFULNESS. Once again, God showered our family with his amazing abundance in healing, joy, in loving family and friends. We humbly receive all these things knowing that it is all about God – not about who I am or who my daughter is – but about how amazing God is. How great thou art. Thank you God!

Do What You Love
and
Love What You Do

Whatever you do, work at it with all your heart, as working for the Lord, not for men. Colossians 3:23

Watching Megan dive is a beauty to behold. Not necessarily because of her skill or ability but because she shines while doing it. You can see how much she loves diving, and it fills my heart with such joy to watch her. I am joyful because she is joyful. If my heart sings while watching my daughter, I can only imagine Gods joy because he loves her so much more.

It makes me realize how important it is to do the things I love, too. Seeing Megan, I must ask myself when do I shine? Where do I see those around me shine? When I see it, I must name it – and be encouraging. Why do we try and change ourselves to fit the world, instead of changing the world to fit who we are? Why do I so often put off my desires and passions because somewhere along the line I have bought into the belief that since I am a parent I must sacrifice all for my children? Why do we women hold each other hostage by constantly saying we must put our children first and deny ourselves? Why have we lost sight of God's abundance? Why can't we see that it is only in our wholeness that we will really be able to give our children freedom? It is only in following our hearts that we will rock this world? It is not about choosing between ourselves OR our children. It is about choosing God and doing both.

We can't be a light to the world if we are always trying to conform to it. If we are trying to change who we are in order to "fill in" we miss out on the greatest gifts God created us to be. If we are spending our days helping at the schools, in church only because they need us – not because our hearts want to be there – then what we are doing is worthless. It is nothing but prideful ego screaming for attention. Unless we free ourselves to listen to our hearts, how can we lead the way? How can we teach our children the true freedom of Christ comes from being the unique child God created them to be – if we are denying that very child ourselves?

You Obey What You Worship

Those who have nothing, but wish they had, are damned with the rich.
For God does not consider what we possess but what we covet
-Saint Augustine

What do I clutch tightly in my hands? What am I unwilling to share? Am I unwilling to share my time to cook my neighbor dinner because I am too busy? Am I crabby because my husband is going to be away three more nights this week to help a friend finish his basement? Am I put out because my parents need help moving a heavy piece of furniture? This too, is coveting something that is not mine – all is Gods.

I usually thought of coveting as wanting or desiring something that is my neighbors. I thought of it as being envious of someone's new purse or coat or car. But another viewpoint surfaced today. What do I covet that I have in my own house or family? What am I unwilling to share? What do I hold tight, not giving generously. Not willing to share my time/talents/possessions is coveting, too, because all these things are Gods.

Do we cherish all that we have been given? Am I thankful for the gifts God has bestowed on me? Out of gratitude do I reach out to bless others?

Julie Maijala Lundquist

You Can Teach An Old Dog New Tricks

No one pours new wine into old wine skins. If he does, the wine will burst the skins, and both the new wine and old skin will be ruined. No, he pours new wine into new wine skins. Mark 2:19-22

Why do so many adults buy into the concept that learning and trying new things must cease after graduation from high school or college? I know so many people who are afraid to try new things. How often do we simply say 'no' to something because we are afraid of looking foolish, or even if we sign up for a class, do we really engage? Do we really try and incorporate what we are being taught into our lives? Do we hear the teaching but let it flow in one ear and out the other, are we afraid of failing, are we afraid of falling? There is much grace in being a beginner. Why have I struggled so hard to constantly move away from that state of grace?

It makes me think about my ski lesson with Franz. For the past few years we have gone skiing in Montana. Every year for Christmas my husband (an expert skier) gives me ski lessons with one of the instructors at Big Sky. I must admit at first I was a little put out – I have been skiing since I was 12 years old and I know how to ski. After deciding not to be grumpy about my gift, I chose to believe Paul gave me lessons because he knows how much I love learning, not because he thought I was a terrible skier. After my first lesson, my ski instructor Franz told me that I should look for skis I could "grow" into. I love that even at age 38 I could continue to become a better skier. To be honest, I had thought maybe I had 'peaked" and I was already skiing at the level I would remain at for the rest of my life. I thought that after skiing for 25 years I had it down. Franz didn't agree. With proper instruction and a willingness to learn I became a better skier. I felt more in control, safer and enjoyed the runs more.

Franz had said he was surprised by my willingness to hear and embrace the new things that he wanted me to work on. People often sign up and pay for lessons but don't really want to learn or change. Many times they do not want to separate from their past habits or make the effort, do the work, to try something different. I think life is like that spiritually, too. We must continue learning all along our journey. We must continually offer up new wine skins (new hearts and open minds) or else we waste what we have been given. We must not only look for the teachers God places for us each day, but we must be open to their teachings.

I can't believe the difference 2 hours of skiing with Franz made in my skiing. I feel more under control, stronger, safer and so much more able to enjoy skiing. I have learned how not to fight against gravity, the hills and on the bumps. I learned how to simply ski. If 2 hours makes such a difference in ski lessons, how can we learn how to live every day not fighting and fleeing from the abundant teachings of God? How can we share with others the joy of living? How can we teach the joy of new wine skins every day?

Vows

I, Julie, take you Paul, to be my husband.
Before God, our family and friends
these things I promise you.

I will be faithful to you and honest with you,
I will trust, care and honor you.
I will love you and cherish you
And I will love you and share
All the days of my life with you.

When Paul and I got married, we decided to write and recite our own vows for our wedding ceremony. We worked on them together and wrote a promise that we were both ready to make. The day of our wedding, I remember thinking it would have been easier to have just gone along with the "regular" wedding vows written in the Lutheran Green Book of worship. There was a lot to remember in our vows, but I worked hard at memorizing the words so I could pledge them out loud. I didn't want to be embarrassed. Luckily, the woman goes first in the vow making. I was happy to have made it through our vows but when it was Paul's turn I could tell he was really nervous. He condensed our promises into one flowing sentence, left out most of it out and spoke them as quickly as he could. I remember knowing he *knew* them and his lapse of memory was not a reflection on his feelings for me. The rest of our day went on without a hitch and we truly enjoyed our day. However, I have often teased him about having forgotten his vows.

Fast-forward 12 years. I had a friendship with another man that was threatening our marriage. Everything was above board. We hadn't broken any rules. It was a casual friendship that involved meeting weekly for coffee to visit about life. Along the way, I discovered we were breaking our spouses hearts. There was something I couldn't quite put my finger on – and neither could Paul – but he was threatened. It was a strange spot to be in because I have so many good male friends and Paul has never felt this way.

One evening as we lay in bed, Paul and I were talking and the topic of our wedding came up. I mentioned something about our wedding vows and his lack of knowing them. I was laughing when Paul rolled over, took my hands and recited our vows as clearly and as perfectly as they had been written 12 years ago. To be honest, I even looked under his pillow for a sheet of paper he may have been reading, but there was nothing but his heart. Paul spoke those words at exactly the right moment and reminded me of what I had promised. Paul may have fumbled with the words on the day we were married but he had clearly written them on his mind and in his heart. He spoke them perfectly the day I really needed to hear them. It was me who had forgotten my vows.

I had been struggling with the question as to whether men and women could be friends. And I found my answer – absolutely they can! As long as I am upholding the vows I made to my husband on my wedding day. In all that say and do, my yes to Paul that day, November 24, 1994 must mean yes, I do! That meant ending a friendship so that we both could honor our vows that we had made before God and our families. It meant acknowledging that a part of me had been thrilled by a friend who thought I was great and would have given me anything I asked for. It meant acknowledging that wanting to help someone else doesn't mean that I am the right person for the job. It meant doing away with one of my life long rules – if you do something out of goodness, it can't be wrong.

I have learned that doing things out of goodness does not make them right. I didn't know that until I read a story about King David. In Chronicles, David wants to move the Ark of the Covenant to Jerusalem. God has decreed all sorts of rules about moving the ark – and David is well aware of them. But he so wants to get this ark moved – maybe simply out of the goodness of his heart –he rushes in and gets the job going. He calls in people to move the ark and they put it on a cart. As the cart is traveling over uneven floor, one of the guides reaches his hand out to steady the ark. He was protecting it from falling. He was doing the "right" thing, but it was the wrong thing. It was against the laws of the Lord. The laws said clearly that no one should touch the ark. The Lord's anger burned against the man and he was struck dead immediately because he had put his hand on the ark. Thank God I wasn't struck down.

I used to ask myself when I had a decision to make " Is this a good thing to do?" Or "Am I doing this out of the goodness of my heart." If I answered yes, then I thought I could proceed. But acting out of goodness isn't always the right thing to do. I think of my friend and our relationship. He needed a friend and was lost. Out of goodness I thought that we could be friends, but I came to realize that our friendship was not good for him or our marriages. Even though it had begun as a way to "steady" his tipping ark – I realized that it wasn't right to continue. After the night Paul spoke our vows from his heart, I saw that I was putting all of our relationships in jeopardy.

The Empty Tomb

But they found the stone rolled away from the tomb. Luke 24:2

Mary did not meet Jesus the Risen Christ until after she found the empty tomb.

Perhaps our life is really about discovering the empty tomb. How do we find it? What does it look like? How do we know where to go? Maybe it is through the guidance of many, or really the guidance of One. Maybe it is in following the compass of our hearts that we learn how to stand holding our heart and our hands open. Maybe it is only then that we can ask Jesus to empty us of our crap. How is it we finally learn we need space in our life, in our souls – not just in our drawers and closets – so we have room to be filled?

Mary did not even recognize him.

Even Mary didn't recognize him. Whew. As humans we are so often blinded to the amazing things God does for us. So often I don't even recognize him. So often I miss seeing the risen Christ in the person behind the check out counter, in the referee at my child's soccer game, or in the solicitor on the phone calling during dinner. How can I better look to truly see Christ in the people in my every day life so that I may respond with love?

Jesus called her by name, and she knew who she was.

Mary was blinded by her grief. Her friend hanging to death on a cross at the far outskirts of town wasn't what she expected. I can't imagine it was anywhere on her radar for "future plans" for her friend. But somehow in her heart she knew she had to go to the tomb, she heard him call her by name. At that moment Mary turned and faced the living, resurrected Living God. This story of discovery is about the truth of transformation. I think it is absolutely amazing. Even Mary gets to undergo a totally transformational change. It is only then that she goes out into the world and tells others. Jesus made sure to reach Mary so she would understand. He appealed to all of her senses – sight, sound, and body, just like he calls out to us today. How can I better listen to the sound of him calling my name? I want to answer and say here I am.

Kilimanjaro

As the deer pants for streams of water, So my soul pants for you, O God. Psalm 42:1

We went as a family last week to watch the Imax movie Kilimanjaro. It is a great story of 8 people who listened to a their hearts calling to climb the mountain. As we watched, we gathered some wanted to climb it because they had never been on a mountain. Others wanted to simply study it, only see if they could do it and some made the climb because they wanted to see if the view from the top was as they had imagined. During the trek they traveled from grassy plains, through the thick rain forest, into the alpine and then onto the rocky region. The guide, a native from Tanzania, had made that same trip more than 250 times. As they traveled, he told the group a story about elephants, panthers and antelopes that had followed this same path over the years, climbing to the very top of Kilimanjaro. The guide knew many different animals had passed through these very places because he had found the remains of some of their bodies. Their remains were often far above elevations these creatures normally lived or even hunted for food. The guide found their bones in the cold, freezing terrain of the mountain that is void of almost all life. At this elevation the mountain is filled with nothing but ice, rock and wind.

After the show, I asked my children why they thought the animals would go to the top of the mountain. Without a pause Mick answered, "To get closer to God." His answer has made me think, and I do believe he is right. All of God's creation so hungers for his presence that we often search and search and search. Sometimes we even find ourselves crawling through rain forests, up rocky hills, and across deserted cold frozen, rocky landscapes. Sometimes our journey is easy going, sometimes it is unimaginably difficult, but that is only part of the story. The other part of the story, the beginning of the story, is God finds us first. God is with us everyday, every step of the way. He is with us every part of our climb. It is his unfailing grace that is always with us and calls out us. It is his grace and presence that we hunger for. It is why Mary went to the tomb. It is why our hearts cry out for something more.

The Race

Do you not know that in a race all the runners run, but only one gets the prize? Run in such a way as to get the prize. Everyone who competes in the games goes into strict training. They do it to get a crown that will not last; but we do it to get a crown that will last forever. 1 Corinthians 9:25

I have been running – and running fast. For some of you that may be no big deal. But, for me, well, it is amazing. I have always been a decent long distance runner, but I have never been quick. I am not sure what is happening but I am finally getting fast. I am not sure why or how even now I am becoming a better runner.

The other day my sister, Miss Speedy Gonzales, saw me running and thought about catching up to me, but I was going too fast to even catch. Then, another one of my friends saw me running past her house and could hardly believe my speed. I hadn't really thought about my pace until then. Over the next weeks many others have asked if I am training for a race and have even suggested that I enter a race and run. The thought was rather unsettling. Me, run a race, for speed? It was quite laughable.

But after some thought, I realized I really was in training. A kind of spiritual boot camp, if you will. Running is one of the few places where I can really drop the crap that gets between God and me. When I run I have no excuses – or else I seem to run out of them pretty fast. In the past few months I have been running and running and running – not thinking about running – but talking with God and listening. I have been focusing on the God while I was running and all of a sudden I am fast. I am learning when we set our hearts eye on we God (long term training) all the other stuff (short term goals) falls into place. I am learning to live with God at the center of all aspects of my life.

No Outlet

For I am convinced that neither death nor life, neither angels nor demons, neither the present or the future, nor any powers, neither height nor depth, nor anything else in all creation, will be able to separate us from the love of God that is in Jesus Christ our Lord. Romans 8:38

Today I noticed a sign that has been on my running route forever, but I just saw for the first time. I saw a sign that said NO OUTLET. This struck me as so amusing that I couldn't help but crack up and laugh out loud as I ran. NO OUTLET. How true – God is constantly working in our lives to bring us closer to him. He is constantly showering us with love, grace and his presence. He works so hard to provide us with no outlet. He wants us to know we can never do anything or go anywhere to get out from under the amazing grace he pours down on us. God is always ready for us, waiting for us whenever we choose to turn to him. He has created our lives to be full beyond our wildest dreams and possibilities. His love for us is so great that he has given us life that screams FULL ABUNDANCE. There is no way out. We have been chosen to be his sons and daughters. We are chosen to be children of God. How blessed we are!

Hemmed In

You hem me in – behind and before; you have laid your hand upon me. Such knowledge is too wonderful for me, too lofty for me to attain. Psalm 139:5-6

God is clearly saying, "I've got your back." He has us covered. He will let us know when we have gone astray. He will let us know of impending danger. God is indeed in front and behind. I have learned this well by playing team sports my whole life – but I didn't realize God was in on it, too.

It's like playing on a team with true friends. I was blessed with playing soccer with a core group of women my entire life. We always knew on the field that wherever we went, whenever we made a run and left our position, whenever we fell back to cover for someone else, another teammate would have our back. We always knew the same rules that applied to games, applied to our lives at school, at work and in our neighborhoods. This same teamwork applies to our faith walk. We are so loved by God and by others. God is watching out for us. That is what this true community, this right relationship with God is all about. It is about being a team, trusting in God and trusting in the goodness of our teammates placed in our lives.

Being hemmed in reminds me that God created us with free will. He isn't bribing us to enter into this rich life by hanging a carrot in front of our noses. Our broken humanness often blinds us to God amazing abundance. Perhaps God has left us with choice because he wants us to experience the true joy of discovering how much he loves us. Perhaps God gives us freedom so that we may experience true joy in Christ. Perhaps he gives us the freedom knowing full well that it is only when two come together that amazing things really do happen. Perhaps God gives us that freedom because he loves to see what great plays we create when we know to trust the One who has our back.

Obedience

*You stiff necked people, with uncircumcised hearts and ears! You
are like your fathers: you always resist the Holy Spirit!   Acts 7:51*

I love mowing, the smell of clipped grass, and the sound of the
mower. I remember my Dad and me mowing together, me standing
beneath his arms helping him push the mower along, carefully watching to
keep one side of the tires in the path of the already mowed lawn so we
wouldn't stray. He taught me well.

I was out mowing our front yard the other day and for some reason I
clearly knew that I should avoid a certain patch of long grass in the corner
near the garden. I "heard" this warning a couple of times each time I
passed this area - and I avoided mowing it. Then, the next time I passed, I
found myself actually arguing about how ridiculous it was for me not to
mow there. I argued that I needed to mow there or else I would have to
stop and walk <u>all</u> the way to the garage (10 feet away) and get the hand
trimmer. It would be so much easier to just mow it and be done.

In an instant I changed direction and cruised over to the corner I knew
I shouldn't mow. I mowed there anyway. What happened next was
horrible. Out came a baby rabbit. A beautiful rabbit scurried away missing
its entire back quarter. I knew as soon as I had pushed my mower in there
that I had been disobedient and then I saw this bunny rabbit. I was
horrified and screamed for Paul. Of course the kids heard my cries and
came running too. I had run over a rabbit. We tried to follow him as the
little rabbit hurried into the back yard and hid. There was nothing we
could do to find him.

I couldn't believe I had known not to mow there and did it anyway. I
couldn't believe that I was so obviously told not to mow there, and I did. I
couldn't believe how disobedient I had been. I prayed for a miracle, for
healing of this little creature. I asked for forgiveness. I prayed that the
little rabbit would not be in pain. I worried all night about the rabbit -
about where he was and how he was doing.

I woke before sunrise the next morning and sat on my front porch swing. As I watched the sun bring the rich warm color of life to my neighborhood, I saw the rabbit's cold dead body lying on the lawn in front of my swing. My heart was filled with sadness. I knew that had I trusted and listened things would have been so much different. I vowed to listen with my whole heart. I vowed not to doubt. I buried the body of the rabbit in my perennial garden under the bleeding heart that was in full bloom.

Julie Maijala Lundquist

Violin

Your people will rebuild ancient ruins and will raise up age-old foundations; you will be called Repairer of Broken Walls, Restorer of Street Dwellings. Isaiah 58:12

A few years ago when I picked the violin back up after a 20 some year hiatus, my teacher placed tape on my strings so I could remember where to place my fingers. Through practice I had "trained my ear" to the sound of those notes. I played music, read music and made music. I thought I was doing great. I really enjoyed playing music again after all those years. I had quit playing my sophomore year in high school, but had missed it. Paul gave me a violin for Christmas a few years ago. After looking at it lie in the case for two years, I finally found enough courage to pick it up.

I had changed teachers over the summer and my new teacher was curious about the difficulty I was having progressing. When she checked the placement of the tape on my strings she found it was in the wrong place. The tape wasn't off by much, but my markers, my guides for playing notes, weren't correct. I had to begin anew to train my ear to the sound of the true notes again. I had to relearn where to put my fingers. I had to learn the true sound of the notes. What a difference it has made. When notes are played in tune the difference is amazing. Anyone who has ever listened to a new musician practicing knows how painful it can be, but when we get it right the sound is just glorious. A note played in tune is clear and strong and crisp. The violin just rings out, YES! This is it! It is good!

I could play music before – but it was often a struggle. I had to work to change my bad habits, but the new sound is amazing, it rings true. How similar this has been to my journey. I was so on track when I was young, but somewhere along the way, the tape was moved on my heart. My guides got out of place. I still made music, but it was a awkward and sometimes just didn't feel right. There was some good stuff going on, but I wasn't shining or ringing out.

138

It is as if I have spent the past 8 years retraining the ear of my heart. I had to pull off the old tape and start over. I have had to unlearn all sorts of bad habits. I have had to learn to listen and to trust. I have had to become vulnerable and humble. I have had to remember how to play in front of people and let my light shine. I have had to remove many obstacles that had led me to stray onto foreign paths. As the tape was pulled off my heart, the highway of God opened up and I have never made such beautiful music before in all my life. It's amazing. I am getting stronger and stronger every day. Not only at the violin, but at most everything. I don't play a symphony, but I hit the right notes so much more often.

And it is not because of my doing; it is because the Lord has blessed my life. It is because I became aware of how out of tune my heart had been. It is because of sheer grace. God pulled the tape off my heart when I laid on the dirt floor of my basement and realized I couldn't go it alone anymore. He then helped me begin to rebuild as he sent amazing people into my life - my three beautiful children. He opened my eyes to the strengths of my husband, family and friends as blueprints to teach and guide me. He has built me new walls, strong and true with the help of amazing friends, family and strangers he has placed in my life. He pulled that tape off and showed me how to rebuild and I have been changed – through no effort of my own concoction or planning. God has made my life ring true.

I found that after playing out of tune for a while, the out of tune sound became my normal. It was close to right but was really nothing like the real thing. It was void of life! I could play music – a little sharp or a little flat – and it may have even sounded (and looked) pretty good but I was missing something. I was lonely. I was homesick.

Today, my life is flooded with amazing grace. It is filled with the love of knowing I will sometimes hit the note right – and sometimes I won't. It is filled with knowing that it isn't about playing the right notes at all – life is about playing with our hearts in the right place. Life and transformation is about grace and our conscious decision to open the door to God. I am so thankful to God for the sheer and total grace of pulling off my tape and not giving up on me. I am so thankful for the encouragement and care of many amazing people in my life. True living rings out strong and clear.

Establish The Work of our Hands

And let the beauty of the Lord our God be upon us, And establish the works of our hands for us; Yes, establish the work of our hands. Psalm 90:17

God directs our purpose and calling. So many times after I had completed a task I have nothing else left to do on my list, but I would find myself creating new jobs to work on. I don't need to "invent" work for my hands to do. I need to trust and believe God has and is establishing the work of my hands this very minute, even right now. Give me courage to see this Lord, and to go through doors you open and accept the chair you offer to simply rest in your presence.

A while ago I got to participate in a weekend retreat that focused on community. We came together prayerfully, choosing to be completely outside of ourselves in order to listen to another's story and questions. Spending time listening with a group of 5 other people was powerfully amazing. It spoke truth on so many levels. I was surprised to see myself in the person speaking. I was surprised to be able to experience another person speak their truth and actually see that our whole group could hear and feel it. It was as if each of us recognized (our true spirit self) the true self, the one, the me, our own being in another. We recognized it again and again as each person spoke, listened or plainly asked a simple question. Jim shed my tears as he spoke; Graham asked a question that I had been journaling about and thinking about in the days before hand. The question laid on Kristin's heart was one of the very same that I had been carrying in mine. We were placed in a group where we belonged.

Today, on my run, I realized that being present occurs on many different ways – physically, spiritually, emotionally and on a multitude of levels. I was thinking about how this world (me) has always placed such a high priority on the physical presence of another – but I am beginning to see that it is equally important to be spiritually present with one another. I had wanted to meet with one of my pastors for many months – just to check in with him to see how was he is doing. For some reason, he was been laid on my heart. I had been asking for a meeting to get together and he did not welcom the invitation because he says he was too busy. A part of me wants to be hurt about that. Thankfully, I realize his unwillingness to meet is not about me. I did not take his rejection personally. Even after his refusal, I find that he is still been laid on my heart. I am learning the truth is that I can be even more influential and helpful by simply praying for his goodness, for God to work in powerful ways, for him to open up to receiving blessings that have been indeed given to him. It IS enough to be present through prayer – while tending to the world that God placed before me physically.

Eli taught me that yesterday. Eli, the perfect baby boy my sister lost before she gave birth. I never met him, never held him, never saw him, never touched him – but I prayed for him and for our family – and because of that I knew him. I still experience his presence and carry him in my heart. As I was driving yesterday I realized how much he had taught me, simply through love in prayer. I love that little boy no differently than my other nieces and nephews I get to play with, send cards to and hug. We are all connected and are all one in the body of Christ.

We are called to be in community physically and spiritually. We are called to come together in prayer, thanksgiving and worship. We are called to unite. We are called to love each other. We are called to bless one another with our presence.

PURPOSE

For it is God who works in you to will and act according to his good purpose. Phillipians 2:13

For it is God who works in us, encouraging us to put time and energy into things we delight in. God instills desire in each of us uniquely. It is a longing he places in our hearts. When we work or act on our passions and desires, we are engaging with God and helping to fulfill his plan here on earth.

I sometimes struggle with what to do with my life. Should I take on more ministry – Alpha, Agora, Marriage Ministry, seminary? I wonder if they are what God has planned for me, or wants me to do. Should I go back to work full time? Should I go back to school? But today I have no heart felt passion for any of them. I have great passion for writing and teaching, volunteering, coaching, playing outside, being with my family and discovering new territories right here in my home as well as all over the world. I have great passion for learning and growing and sharing my joy.

What a relief. We don't need to stress about "should." We don't need to constantly worry about what we should do. God's world is about living by heart. It is about listening to the passion that God placed in your heart. The Lord will fulfill his purpose for each of us. Trusting in God takes away the anxiety and worry of making sure we are doing the right thing. When we are in tune with God and inviting him into our daily lives, that our my work. We must listen and trust that the Lord WILL fulfill his purpose for us. We must believe that his promises are true and have the courage to take a step forward over and over.

This is why we must follow our heart and our true longings – because they are gifts from God. They may even be markers on our map. Maybe even our desires and passions make up the compass that points the direction of our hearts to moments that give us glimpses of heaven on earth! Maybe our stirrings and longings are exactly that, like rocks people pile up in the forest to mark the way of a path, to direct us along our highway, from strength to strength until we are home.

A Highway

And a highway shall be there; It will be called the Way of Holiness. Isaiah 35:8

I have always held tightly to the idea that 'the path is narrow and only a few find the way'. I have carried this image of a tightrope in my heart ever since I have been a child. I really wanted to be one of the chosen but I was so afraid of falling off the tightrope and failing. Too often, I was afraid that God would force me to walk the narrow road. I wanted no part of it. It seemed all too scary.

I am learning that God promises a highway for the remnant of his people. This path is nothing to fear. God calls us past the rules, past "should" and "have to" to compassion and love. He called to me and a highway opened up. The road is high and broad, posted with signs and markers, and sometimes even mile markers. We only have to trust that these are the very things right in front of our noses. When we don't see them, we must trust that we are on the path and God is guiding us. God does indeed provide for us a highway. True living is living on the highway - and I want to ride it all life long.

Thanksgiving

***For this is God, our God forever and ever; He will be our guide
even to death. Psalm 48:14***

Uncle Arden and Aunt Freda came up to celebrate Thanksgiving. We
talked of "old times" and reminisced about family gatherings with all the
cousins (almost 50 of us!). Uncle Arden laughed as he said I could do no
wrong in my cousin Todd's eyes – and still can't. Todd and I grew up
together playing in the woods by the Raccoon River, building tree houses,
telling each other our secrets, listening to Billy Joel on his sisters record
player as she pounded on her locked bedroom door trying to get in. Uncle
Arden's comment made me smile because I love my cousin very much.
He is one of those people that I can go years without seeing or talking to
and still fall into step immediately when we get together. He has always
been like a brother to me and I am very thankful for our relationship.

When I became interested in boys, some of my dating experience fell
short because of the great relationship I had with my cousin Todd. I
learned a lot about what love is – and what it is not. I learned it was vital
to marry a man who would love me dearly and wholly and was someone I
could love the same in return. I learned how important it was to play and
run and laugh. I learned how great it was to be a team, even if our only
opposition was our little sisters. I believe that it may have been my
experience with my cousin Todd that kept me on track while I was dating-
and I didn't even realize it until I took a look back while Arden and I were
talking. That's what I am talking about. Even then God provided me with
a highway in my youth for my future as a wife.

On earth As It Is In Heaven

Our Father which art in heaven, Hallowed be thy name. Thy kingdom come, thy will be done in earth, as it is in heaven. Give us this day our daily bread. And forgive us our debts, as we forgive our debtors. And lead us not into temptation but deliver us from evil; for thine is the kingdom and the power and the glory, forever. Amen.

What if the focus of living is less on where we go when we die and more about which world we choose to live in today? What if the power of Christ, what if the prayer we pray when we say the Lord's Prayer is all about living NOW?

Thy kingdom come. Thy will be done on earth as it is in heaven. This prayer doesn't say "will come" or "comes" but uses the present tense of the verb. We are asking God's kingdom to come today, on earth, in every aspect of our lives. If we get stuck thinking that life is all about earning our way into heaven do we miss out? Is it really more important trying to earn admission than to live a life filled with love and compassion? If we don't believe the basic truth that we can't earn our way in, do we miss out on the journey?

Does this perspective change the way I live today? Does it change my actions? I believe it does. Christ guarantees we will see him again in heaven. I believe that with all of my being. But I think he wants more for us. I believe Christ has another gift in mind for us. Heaven, now, on earth. That's transcendence or transformation.

Christ asks us to let our light shine. He doesn't say, "Show your neighbor what you've got." He simply says to get out of the way and let your light shine. You have been created uniquely magnificent. Your light is different from any one else's here on earth. The most amazing way to call out the light in others is to let your own light shine. He is not asking us to show our neighbors what we've got. I think that means not worrying about the quality, color or make and model of light. That means quit looking at what everyone else is doing, comparing and judging and just let your light shine.

I love the end of concerts. I love the end of the show when the lights go out and the crowd comes alive. They cheer and whistle. Together, strangers jammed into an auditorium listening with wonder and awe, unite their voices and whistles in praise for the show. They join and celebrate the amazing gift the musicians shared. One by one, lighters are flicked on and held into the darkness. The crowd chants "Just one more. Just one more." It is a progression but it's catchy and soon the entire auditorium is filled with voices and illuminated by small individual lights.

I have never been to a concert and heard one person tell another that they couldn't let their light shine because it wasn't the same as theirs. I have never heard of anyone not holding out their lighter because it was different that the rest. I can't even imagine the musicians would even care what kind of light it was – just that it was shining. Who wouldn't want to hear "We want more! You are amazing"? You see if I believed life was all about what happened at the end, I would miss it. I would miss the amazing music and the concert itself. I would miss living. Maybe I would become judgmental – and the Pharisee in me would judge my own light and the light of my neighbors.

But, if I believe life is about bringing heaven to earth here, today, I am held more accountable. Honestly, I have so much to watch out for in my own life that I really don't have time to judge anyone – myself included. God created us to glorify him – not because he is an egotistical maniac but because he knows that living every minute of every day to glorify him has much LESS to do with sacrificing our lives (God always asks what do you want?) and more to do with the total freedom of living in God's amazing world. It has everything to do with wonder and joy and love and peace and abundance.

Living this way brings about transformation. It changes not only my life but also the lives of everyone in my world. If I hold up my light, suddenly my entire world becomes transformed. It becomes shot through with heaven. (Thy kingdom come, thy will be done on earth as it is in heaven.) My entire world is like the end of a concert. You can see it, you can feel it, and you can smell it and taste it.

It isn't just a one-time shot. Jesus doesn't just give us one more song. Jesus is telling us it is the way to live. Now. Today. And every day for the rest of your life. Knowing full well, that God, the musician and the artist, in his amazing grace will continue coming out from backstage. He will continue to play and create an amazing world for us to live in. Unlike the musicians of our world, God isn't offering just a one or two song encore. He keeps playing and longs for you and I to have the courage to be willing to ask. And we give great thanks and praise by letting our lights shine. Don't worry; when the concert of life is finally over, I do believe God does indeed hold out on playing the greatest song for the very end. There is something to be said about saving the best for last!

Believing is Seeing

Now faith is being sure of what we hope for and certain of what we do not see. Hebrews 11:1

If you don't first believe you may never see. That is why the statement "If you change your attitude, you change your life" is so true. If you don't believe in God's presence in the ordinary, even in the "mundane" you may never see it. If you don't believe in present day miracles, you may never see them.

People say great things happen when you least expect them. But I think the greater truth is too often in our "ordinary and routine" life we *expect* to find exactly what we have always seen. This belief limits our views on miracles, it limits our ability to see and recognize God's awesomeness and His great presence. To live our freedom in this amazing and abundant world we must get outside ourselves and love God, neighbor and enemy. We must open our eyes and our hearts to God's amazing kingdom and not limit our life by what we have already experienced.

We do this not by forcing. We do this by being fully present and outside ourselves. That's when heaven breaks through to earth, not because of anything we have done, but through God's sheer grace and our lives become transformed. The awesome part of living this way is that not just our own person but also every single relationship in our life, marriage, family, friends, finances, neighbors, nature, becomes transcended. What happens is not just a transformation of an individual, but also a renewal of our entire our world? It is the recreation of a whole a new world. It is amazing.

Time

Therefore I say to you, whatever things you ask when you pray, believe that you receive them, and you will have them. Mark 11:24

I'm not so sure God's time is so different from ours. I think maybe the difference has to do more with our sight than it does with minutes ticking on a clock. Time is really all about faith and trust and belief. God doesn't make us wait. He is always standing on the other side of the door waiting for us to invite him in. There is no distance for him to travel. He waits. Ask. He will answer now.

Walls

The temple had a wall around it, 500 cubits long and 500 cubits wide, to separate the holy from the common. Ezekiel 42:20

O.K. I'll admit it. I have spent a good part of my life thinking that my life was better than, well, yours. That is, if you kept little tyke primary colored plastic gear in either your living room or dining room, camped in a pop up tent, or ever walked your dog at one of those fenced in dog parks. I mean, please. I am more of the eccentric adventurous type. Who needs any more of those fenced in eyesores in the world? Well, thank you Jesus, for never ever giving up on me.

I had been humbled before. After three kids, I knew very well what it was like to sacrifice every part of my home to the blast of toddler toys. I actually came to see those very bold colors as life saving blessings helping me to entertain my little monsters! And the tent, ever tried camping with a three kids and a dog for 10 days in a small lightweight 4-man tent? I will be the first to tell you that those pop up campers are a tremendous aid in enjoying the out of doors. But today, let me tell you about my most recent hold out – dog parks.

I am a runner. I love adventure. I have two big dogs and they love to run off leash. So, you would think that I have tried bringing them to one of those new fangled Pet Exercise Areas before. Nooo, not someone as pig headed as me. No way you would have found me in one of those small, confined, fenced in, RESTRICTED areas. Well, for some glorious reason, I went today. I tried not going, but I knew in my heart I needed to go. Guess what? It blew my socks off. I loved it, the dogs loved it. It was so, well, freeing!

It really made me think of turning my life over to Christ. I struggled with the whole concept of turning my life over. I was afraid of all the restrictions, and the changes that God would make me do. Frankly, I didn't want to get in any more trouble. And I knew from past experience that is where I had already spent enough of my time, in trouble, but a cool thing happened. I turned it over and it was amazingly freeing.

While I was walking the dogs in the dog park today, I couldn't help but compare the two things. The dogs ran freely...and I swear they were smiling. They did their own dog things. I saw their "personalities" shine out. Rookie ran ahead and greeted every one while Duchess hung back and just enjoyed the smells. The dogs weren't aggressive towards others. Even Rookie and his big male dog ego, there wasn't any posturing, he just wanted to play. It was as if he knew he was safe there. They were simply radiant.

That's what life in Christ is like. So many people I talk with speak of not wanting to give up the control. They are afraid of what will happen to them. Honestly, it really is like a walk in the (dog) park. Life with Christ is most freeing. His goodness and grace calls out the gifts that each one of us has been given. You should have seen my dogs out there today fully enjoying life. I know some people like that, too, living in the grace and freedom that only Christ can give. That is what transformation is all about. It is about being open to the abundance that God wants to offer us each and every day. And some days, that might even mean going to the dog park. The truth WILL set you free.

Making Time

You have made known to me the ways of life; you will make me full of joy in Your presence. Acts 2:28

These past few years seem as if God has blessed me with an abundance of time. Sometimes I think my days have 100 hours in them. But that description isn't really right. It is really just as if I had looked at time like this (a flat clock), but now time seems to have rolled on it's side and looks more like a chandelier with these long amazing jewels that hang down throughout the day (what I would call little bits of heaven). Now this doesn't happen every day – but it is far more normal than it is not.

It is as if when I choose to stay fully present, (not trying, but asking) the hours, the seconds and the minutes are so much richer and filled with details of smells, sights and sounds. My days are deeper and wider. It is as if time got more multidimensional. People often ask me how I have time to do all that I do – I don't have an answer. God does. I am learning to let my days unfold. Things that need to get done get done – as well as even more amazing things that God has planned for me that day. These "extras" are usually things that weren't even on my radar screen at the beginning of the day but often wind up being the most glorious part of my day.

I have found it easier, the letting go, the unplugging my bathtub part and letting the grime flow out down the drain, when I do the these two things. (Think of this as the Julie Maijala Lundquist life manual – mine and mine alone, I share it with you in case it makes any sense. This is not **the** right way, this is just my story.)

1. Love God with all my heart, soul, mind and body.
2. Love others (neighbors, enemies and myself)

This means start out every day walking with God. Sometimes that means prayer, meditation or an early morning run. Sometimes that means sitting quietly alone, early before any one else gets up. Sometimes that means throwing off the covers and running for the shower, all the while giving God thanks for this glorious day. Most days it means cracking open the book of truth and wisdom and allowing God to speak to me through his powerful word. I have learned the importance of listening directly to the Holy Spirit through the Word, without another author involved. As tempting as it is to always read the Best Seller list, go directly to the source, the Holy Scripture, for current and up to date information and advice.

Go outside every day. Life is so amazing when we leave the confine of our houses and get out in the fresh air. Make time everyday to breathe. Working out in a gym does not count. Wearing music headphones does not count. We need fresh air. We need space in our hearts, in our minds, in our ears. We must walk with God everyday. If we are too busy to walk with God, we are not living. When outside, open your eyes. Look for the beauty that surrounds you. It is everywhere. See and experience God in nature. Get close to a tree, look at the roots, feel the texture of the bark, listen to the leaves in the wind. Allow your heart and soul to wonder.

Ask God to show you his face in everything and everyone you meet. Simply love. Choose with intent to live. We must choose to live in praise and thanksgiving for the absolute abundance in our life. If we can't see it, ask to see it. Ask for the Lords help to open your eyes. Then look, listen. Shut up and listen to what others (and God!) have to say. Listen to him speak to you of his great love for you and all people. Then, when it is your turn to speak, tell your story and no one else's. Get out of the way and let God's light shine.

Play

You will go out in joy and be led forth in peace; the mountains and hills will burst into song before you, and all the trees of the field will clap their hands. Isaiah 55:12

I went snowboarding with my husband the other day and we had such a great time. I had forgotten how much I love playing with him. We spent a couple hours on the hill and just enjoyed the ride. He has always made me laugh and I am so thankful to God for this man. What a partner - encouraging, joyful and so very loving.

Last week our relationship took a great step forward, too. I am so glad we are still learning how to improve our marriage. One day I had fallen off track and was not very loving. I had gotten crabby, stressed, argumentative, and honestly I just wanted to fight. Every cupboard I opened seemed as if a bomb had just gone off, my calendar weighed 1200 pounds with obligations, and I was looking for bad and barking at the kids.

Paul was so great. He held his ground. He stood in the light and did not get pulled off course by me. We had gotten into a bad habit of allowing me to be the emotional thermometer in our house. If Momma's mad, everybody better run and scurry. If Mommas stressed, walk on eggshells. If Momma's ticked off, Paul found things to get ticked off about, too. A few weeks ago we talked about how awful it was living like that. I explained to Paul that I needed him to stand firm in the light when I was running for the darkness. This time he did just that. He didn't reprimand or get down on me. He simply stood in the light – and it was enough to turn me around. His goodness and love caught me red handed and I felt my heart swing back around like a boomerang. That's what letting your light shine can do. That's what God can do – the light won my day.

The Way It is

There is a thread you follow. It goes among
Things that change. But it doesn't change.
People wonder about the things you are pursuing.
You have to explain about this thread.
But it is hard for others to see.

While you hold it you can't get lost.
Tragedies happen; people get hurt
Or die; and you suffer and grow old.

Nothing you can do stop times unfolding,
But you don't ever let go of the thread.
-William Stafford

I heard it through the grape vine the other day that I am one "laid back parent." What a crack up. I have always thought myself to be on the stricter side of things. Surprisingly, this revelation did not sit well with me. I was shocked to find out how much I still cared what other people thought of me.

I was caught off guard because I didn't want anyone judging my children or me and thinking I let them run around like crazy hooligans. When I hear "laid back parenting," I think "out of control kids." To be honest, my pride was dented. I really work hard (pray, pray, pray for God's help). I thought parenting was something that had been going pretty well (by God's grace) in our house. In my head, laid back says "not caring, not paying attention." Perhaps this is what "unfolding " looks like. Perhaps it looks effortless trusting in someone much greater than myself. Maybe allowing God to work in our life, allowing God to work in the lives of our children, and getting out of the way to allow Christ to love looks easy. I can attest it is one of the hardest things I have ever tried to do in my whole life.

My ego still wants to make it known that I am a good Momma. My ego wants to focus on me and how much time and effort I put into this thing called parenting. But the work and effort involved in raising children is the same as it is for all other endeavors. It is simply loving God with our whole hearts and loving our children as ourselves. It is getting out of the way and allowing God to work through us. My work is turning to the Lord in all things. It is choosing to lay it down (my ego, stress, worries) and to live in joy. When that is done maybe it looks effortless. Maybe it looks real laid back.

Anything but Ordinary....

Then Jesus said to them, "Follow me, and I will make you become fishers of men." Mark 1:17

We are created to live a life that is anything but ordinary. For a long time I thought following Jesus meant "going" someplace or "doing" something great. Jesus <u>is</u> constantly telling us to follow him, but it so much more than just the direction our feet are heading. I love how in Matthew a man on the road tells Jesus he will follow him wherever he goes. Jesus replies 'Foxes have holes, birds of the air have nests, but the Son of Man has nowhere to lay his head." In other words, following Jesus is NOT a destination, it is a journey. Following Jesus is a life way, the true way of living. He offers an amazing way of living that changes my life, your life, and my neighbor's life into anything but ordinary.

I remember standing in my kitchen a couple springs ago, looking out the window and marveling at this big beautiful robin that was perched in our maple tree. Granted, I live in Minnesota and tend to get a little over excited about any sign of spring, but really, the beauty took my breath away. I pointed out the beauty of this amazing bird and was struck by my guests reply. She was put out because I was excited about a "simple old plain robin." "That's nothing special", she said, "just an ordinary old bird."

It broke my heart to hear her say that. I was so very sad for what she was missing. I was so very sad for me too, for the beauty and goodness in this world that I have been so often blind to. That afternoon we didn't talk anymore about birds but the blueprint of the story has stayed with me. I often think about the changes that happened in my ordinary life when I gave God my heart. Following him has been a journey filled with depth and breadth and riches beyond any I had ever imagined.

Living a life anything but ordinary isn't about checking off goals, stressing about getting the right job, living in the right house, or scheming and planning about the future. It is quite the contrary. It is simply about showing up, exactly where you are each and every moment. It is about trusting God with your life and settling down. The hard work in this life way is not about muscling your way into a new life, but rather allowing God to unfold his plans for you moment by moment. For me, it meant learning I was too prideful and wanted to do something great and big and huge and complicated and lots of work, work, work (read here: Look how great I am).

God tells us He created all things and we know his creation is good. I know I have to be careful not to look at my own life like my guest did that spring day when she looked out the window and said "that's nothing special, it just an ordinary old bird." There are so many times I look at my life and think – that's nothing special. So, you sell software, you coach, you volunteer at school, you are the President of the PTC (don't even admit that one), that's nothing great. You're not a doctor, or a scientist, or a teacher, or a missionary saving starving children. You are just a plain old girl. But see, if that is how I live my life, if that is the truth I choose to believe, there isn't place for Christ. Because he came to save me, save you, save all of his creation from death. Christ promises a life that is anything but ordinary.

I can only tell you my story. Take a look out your window. I mean really look. What do you see? Try it; allow the beauty of creation to sink in. Marvel at it. Invite the love and the light of Christ to shine before your eyes. Close your eyes and ask again. Now open them. Welcome to the family, I am so excited for you to live your life, a life that is anything but ordinary.

Crayons

"And you shall know the truth, and the truth shall make you free." John 8:32

Every year when September rolls around I love going to the stores and looking at all the school supplies. I have always been excited about a fresh year, clean tablets, sharp pencils and brand new color crayons. Do you remember the smell, the texture, and the taste? The way the paper that wraps around crayons is thicker and rougher than you expected? I love how crayons always leave beautiful colors – sometimes light and translucent, sometimes dark, waxy and bold. New crayon edges are so crisp, so clear – so unblemished. A new box of crayons reminds me of the perfection God sees in me.

Too often, I feel like the used, broken, dirty, partially unwrapped chunk of crayon lying in the bottom of the old shoebox. Simply tossed aside and disregarded because my wrapper is peeling, my edges are worn and I am not quite as shapely as I used to be.

But God's abundance is great. He takes us in any condition and loves us fiercely. His great love tells us we are not broken. Jesus tells us that we have been set free. He tells us to stand ourselves up and shake the dust from our feet. He tells us to move and color this world.

God calls us to come bearing gifts for others everyday. Through your work, commitment, strength, joy, courage and color inspire others to experience the newness of each and every moment. Call them out to let their light shine. Like sunlight streaming through cut crystal, we are called to leave our mark on the world.

Child

It is right that we should make merry and be glad, for your brother was dead and is alive again, and was lost and is found. Luke 15:32

I was out walking one morning and remembered something I felt very strongly a few years ago. I would wake early and walk the dogs in the park and a strange feeling overwhelmed me. I felt as if I would round a corner someday and find a child. I saw in my minds eye that I would find a child just waiting for me to take home and nourish and love. I had forgotten all about that image for a long, long, long time. Funny how today, while I was out walking in the woods, I knew the child I had been looking for was found. As I was out in the woods searching for moss under fallen logs, I knew it was true – and that very child was me!

I don't know how it happened or why, but I do know without a doubt that my child self had been found. As I was playing, living and walking in the woods, this overwhelming sense of joy came over me because I knew it to be true. I was lost and now am found. I am so very thankful to God for finding me and keeping me and leading me back home.

I think that I had just so lost myself. I had forgotten how to play, how to live and how to follow my heart. I had forgotten to dwell. I had forgotten how to really love. Walking with Jesus changed all that. It opened my eyes and my ears and my heart to new beauties and discoveries. My life has gotten so much deeper, richer and fatter. As I grew into who I have become (or maybe more truthfully, who I have always been) I became who I really was meant to be.

Miracles

Ephphatha!

When we read the gospels we see over and over again that Jesus heals all those who touch him. If we need a miracle, we must come in contact on some level with Jesus, God or the Holy Spirit. The truth is there must be a willingness to accept the gift, or an openness to receive or listen. We must believe. Maybe RECEIVING in faith is just as important as giving.

Jesus own words in Mark commands "Ephphatha!" It means be opened! What needs to be opened? Maybe it is heaven, our ears, our heart and soul. We need to be open to create space to receive the gift, to understand the teaching, to hear the message. We must believe and be open to experience miracles in our lives.

Choose with Intent

...and this water symbolizes the baptism that now saves you also – not the removal of dirt from the body but the pledge of a good conscience towards God. It saves you by the resurrection of Jesus Christ. 1 Peter 3:21

I had a day of hard travel. Due to close connections and slight delays I missed my flight. Most of the people trying to make connections accepted our delay gracefully, but many became downright rude and foul mouthed. I chose to stand in goodness. I had to make a conscious choice, because I really was disappointed to have missed my connection. It meant that I would be late for a conference I was so looking forward to attend. I didn't want to miss a thing, but I made a conscious choice to stand in joy and hopefulness. That was work for me, this day.

Questions

Call to me and I will answer you and tell you great and unsearchable things you do not know. Jeremiah 33:3

I think about that day when I was putting away laundry (ordinary!) a few years ago. I remember that thought came into my mind about giving Jesus my whole life. Why was I so stinking afraid to do that? How did this question get there? Why? Why did I decide to ask it? Because it was only then, while walking a path I had walked hundreds of times, doing a task that I had done just as many times, moving back and forth from my closet to my dresser – that I knew I must – or maybe that I had to, because there was no other choice. It was what I wanted – to give my ALL to Christ. That day was a signpost.

ALLULAH

For God so loved the world, that he gave his only begotten Son, that whosoever believes in him should not perish, but have everlasting life. John 3:16

I met a great man in Austin named Allulah. His name means "Great Warrior." He came to this country from Ethiopia when he was 16. As I was riding in the back of his cab, I listened to his story of how his parents wanted him and his siblings to come to the U.S. because of his country's war, famine, and political unrest. I thought of how difficult it must have been for his parents to send their children off to a place they had never been, or may never see, knowing full well they may never see their children with your human eyes again.

I don't know if I could be strong enough to let my children go. I am so often prideful thinking I can make their life better or full. I so often think that if they are with me or are in my care they will be safe and all will be well. I pray I will be strong enough like Mary the Mother of Jesus and Allulah's mother, to send my child into the unknown. I pray that I will be strong enough to risk losing my child so they could find renewed life. That is true parenting.

Love Circles

Every valley shall be exalted and every mountain and hill brought low; the crooked places shall be made straight and the rough places smooth. Isaiah 40:4

I met a friend who is a watercolor painter. She has been working on improving her technique in painting people and she passionately explained to me one day while we were out taking a walk that there are no angular lines in the human body. I wonder, what shapes did she see in the ones she loves? She spoke of swoops and curves of the human body and while we were talking I looked up and there were 4 turkey vultures riding the air currents overhead. They were riding the wind and dancing in circles over the hills of Austin.

Perhaps my own angles and sharp edges I have been afraid of and worried others might see have never been there at all. Could they have been just the sharp edges of my own fear of not being good enough? Could they have been the sharp edges the Pharisee in my heart wanted to call out? Love most certainly is a circle. It is whole, complete and engaged in other, without edges.

Trust

If you fear, put all your trust in God: that anchors holds.

How often I have misused the word trust and used it as manipulation for things I wanted to be in control or in charge of. To the kids "I trust you will pick up the house tonight." Which really meant "you better pick up the house tonight." To my husband "I trust that you will be home from work by 6:00," which really meant if you are not home by 6:00 I will be angry. But trust is a whole other thing completely. It is about the power of loving goodness for another and knowing that God is indeed working to bring about good for all of us, all the time. It is about letting go, not in an "I give up" sort of way, but rather in a hope filled, heartfelt "I believe" kind of way.

The Bach Principle

I play the notes, in order, as they are written.
It is God who makes the music.
-Johan Sebastian Bach

I met a man who lives on Canyon Road in Sante Fe who shared with me the power of the Bach principle. Bach wrote amazing music. He knew how to tell a story with notes and rests. David, my new friend, taught me that Bach had identified this principle by writing music that allowed musical notes to be played slowly. When he did this, Bach allowed each note to create a life of its own, in full relationship with the notes that surrounded it.

David is a musician, too, and we were talking about how he finds it more difficult to play notes slowly. There is a natural tendency to run through music sometimes like a freight train. I could understand what he was talking about. So often, I live my life like that. The Bach Principle is one that encourages the musician to play each note on its own. In doing so, the musician gives each note the freedom to almost conduct themselves. It takes courage to play each note for its fullness. It takes courage to rest in silence between the stanzas. It takes great training to play a note to completion and then rest. Without these spaces, the rests, the music doesn't hold its shape. It doesn't have life. It doesn't resonate and commune with the listener. It doesn't give us the room for the seed to take root and grow.

I can see this in my experience with the violin. I tend to rush through music, almost as if I am afraid of the individual notes by themselves. But to truly play, to truly live, we must allow each day, each experience and each note to sound forth. Our restraint gives freedom to our life; it creates space for truth to tell the whole story. Being present with each note like this in our life allows each experience to be deep and rich and full.

Dwell

Trust in the Lord and do good; Dwell in the land and enjoy safe pasture. Delight yourself in the Lord and he will give you the desires of your heart. Psalm 37:3-4

Running past the horses today I noticed they were so filled with beauty and strength. It was an amazing spring day, the kind of day that settles into your heart and flutters like the wings of a butterfly. I was surprised to see horses lying down in the green pasture, besides the still water of the pond. These great lumbering beasts were lying on their sides. At first I thought they might be sick or tired but then I noticed all 7 of them were lying down in the glorious sunshine amidst the morning dew in the bright spring green grass. With ears alert, they rested. They lived strongly and boldly. I saw an enormous amount of praise in their strong muscles as they rested in God's amazing world. As I watched them I realized how very little I allow myself to do that.

When I finished my run I headed into our backyard and sat in my green plastic Adirondack chair. I rejoiced in the glory of this world, God's great creation. I sat amongst the spring peepers croaking their praise, the smell of wet soil and new growth and I witnessed amazing things. I felt like Snow White as beautiful blue heron flew overhead and chickadees landed near. Squirrels ran right under my chair and rabbits came out from their nest (in my garden, of course!) and explored the day. What abundance, what beauty. I was so amazed at all these things I saw new in my backyard that morning that I had never seen before. It was truly as if I was given new eyes to see my old landscape, a place I had inhabited for the past 8 years and have missed so much! What a blessing to see, to live, to dwell.

Fragments

Remember the Sabbath and keep it holy. Exodous 20:8.

If we don't honor our commitments our lives can become fragments. If we say "yes" too often we may not have time to fully learn what we really want. We may not play each note, each experience as intended. With out any quiet down time, doing nothing time, we have no idea what we are missing and yearning for. Being fragmented never allows for us to fully experience the gift at hand if we are always leaving early or coming late.

Am I over committing my calendar? Am I over committing my children's schedules so they have no time to play? Am I honoring my life with space for rest? Are we running from appointment to appointment without time to breathe? Are we playing each note fully, allowing ourselves to live preciously in each moment? Are we allowing rest in our days, giving our hearts time to pause, creating space to grow into? Are we really honoring our Lord of the Sabbath?

Enough

The Lord is my portion, says my soul, Therefore I trust in him.
Lamentation 3:24

Is *this* enough? Is *it* enough? I seem to wake with this question...if this is all I have, is it enough? Is it enough if my son is never the super star baseball or soccer player? If my daughter never is homecoming queen or ever is in the gifted and talented program? Is it enough if my children don't get invited over to the "popular" neighbors house? Is it enough if we never get the cabin up north, travel to Africa, or build a bigger house? Is it enough if my husband's company never goes public? Is it enough if I never get a book published or never am invited to speak at any functions? Is it enough to live each day knowing how much God loves me and cares for me? Is it enough waking each day and following God – in all the details of my ordinary life? Is it enough to turn and look outside the windows of my heart and love my neighbor as myself? Is it enough to simply allow myself to grow into the child of God I was created to be?

I am realizing that in order to walk on the true and narrow path, the answer must first be yes. God is enough. God is way more than enough. My job, my work, is to this very day lay my worry, pride, ego and self-centeredness down at the foot of the cross. And then turn and live exactly where I am in the hope and joy and peace of Christ. I am realizing that I must do both of these things – lay them down and turn and face the light and the life in Christ. To live is to truly know and trust God is in control and has a plan for my life. Yes, to know God and to love him, that is enough.

Unbelief

"I do believe. Help me overcome my unbelief."   **Mark 9:24**

What if someone told you they wanted to give you an all expense paid trip to Hawaii? Would you turn it down? Accept it? I was offered just that gift – and I told my husband it "just wouldn't work" because the dates were all wrong. I would have to move too many things around and the kids would have to miss another week of school. But the idea, the gift, laid on my heart. I really wanted to see Hawaii. I have never been there and have heard glorious things about it. But, the gift didn't fit into my time line. I wanted March. March 26-April 3, to be exact. This gift was for the first week of May. The nerve.

But on my run today I was thinking about unbelief, which shows up in so many ways in my life. I saw how my unbelief challenges me to not accept gifts I have been given because a part of me believes that I can't accept them, or in this case, I was afraid my husband didn't deserve it (but do we ever?). Or perhaps I thought I shouldn't accept the gift because then maybe he could lose his job. In Mark, Jesus commands, "Be opened!" It's hard to tell if he is commanding the deaf man's ears, tongue, the heavens or his heart. I think maybe he was commanding all of them. I heard it today, loud and clear – be opened! Guess what, I am going to Hawaii…and forgive me for my unbelief.

Leader

But just as he who called you is holy, Be holy in all you do.
1 Peter 1:15

My dear friend asked me today "What kind of leader are you?" I was taken aback by her question – and even more surprised by my conclusion.
I let my light shine.
I reflect the light of those around me.
I name and call out goodness.
I know my own limitations and rely on the gifts of others for wholeness.
I am strong.
I love.
I have endurance.
I am passionate.
I play hard.
I wear out my shoes.
I am creative.
I have a compass.
I am humorous.
I see the big picture.
I can see.
I can hear.
I can feel.
I teach.
I am compassionate.
I encourage.
I train.
I support.
I have a voice.
I am free.
I am an artist.
I am alive.

I heal.
I build up others.
I know justice, mercy and truth.
I befriend.
I welcome.
I am a follower.

Advent

You also, like living stones, are being built into a spiritual house to be a holy priesthood, offering spiritual sacrifices acceptable to God through Jesus Christ. 1 Peter 2:5

I went for a run today. The cold wind blew against my cheeks, jolting me back to the reality that I actually live in Minnesota. As I ran through a subdivision not far from my house, I felt the sob coming up from my soul before tears broke to the surface of my cheeks. Not sure of my sorrow, I continued, feet pounding the pavement, quieting down my soul and listening. A big question came floating into my heart...if Jesus is indeed the rock, the boundary stone in my life (and I answered a whole resounding Yes!), then what about church? Do I need church? What is church? Why do I want church?

In reading Acts, Luke tells us about living the Way – he mentions prayer, breaking of bread, fellowship and teaching. These are the four areas that a new church in our area is concentrating their community on. I have been asked to be a part of the leadership team and I am one stressed out leader. The church is a missional plant church for the ELCA to go and grow a church with the same theology but different methodology. I am really excited about the concept of a church without walls – so excited in fact that I could be the poster child for this type of movement. But what I am beginning to question – because I need to know for myself, why are we doing this?

My calendar is beginning to fill up with meetings, potluck dinners, caroling events and family get to know you dinners. It is as if someone has laid an entire other persons calendar over my life. A life I have worked so hard to let go of, a life that contains space and margin, a life that allows me the freedom to fly. A life that I only had found again after letting go of so much of the orchestration and planning and scheming and control that I managed to grip so tightly throughout my early thirties. And now, the new church plant, with focus on right relationship and building community, is strapping a corset on my heart and I am finding it harder and harder to breathe.

I am really trying to understand my feelings of constraint. If living a life in the path of Jesus is what we are called to do – if it really is about loving God with all my heart, body and soul and loving my neighbor and my enemies – where does a church and walls come in? If I am living a life as true as possible (knowing and acknowledging that I screw up along the way) but still focused on Jesus, and have made and continue to make a choice to live right relationship with everyone that I meet, I live a life of life of teaching and prayer and breaking of bread – how am I supposed to pick up this life I have now and squeeze it into a box called "new church without walls"? It seems so much smaller than my life today – it seems so much more crowded. It seems conventional and conforming.

What if my voice to step out of leadership at my current church community was a voice calling me to step back from all areas of "institutional" leadership. Maybe it was a call to concentrate on right living leadership. Maybe it was a small voice calling out that I need fresh air and trails and trees – not more planning and saving dates on my calendar. Maybe I was crying out because I was flying again, freely, after all these years and didn't want to be tethered to anything but God. Maybe the tears crashed to the surface today because I think that I am on to something. Maybe the tears were the only way my true self could be heard because the words don't even make sense. Maybe the concept of a church without walls sounds like more freedom, but true freedom is found in rebuilding the walls.

Maybe too often the "leader" in me looks to the future - counting the headlights of the cars in my own funeral processional – measuring the "success" of my life not simply by loving wholly and completely, but by how much and by how many I was loved. Maybe this child of my heart doesn't want to be the one in charge managing a direction set by something other my heart. Quite frankly, so often I don't have a clue; the only thing that I have to trust is that the Lord will never let me go. Sometimes, just sometimes, I might hear a small voice calling out of the dessert " prepare ye the way of the Lord." And today, I can't possibly think about preparing for the Lord if my days are packed with meetings and running and deadlines and temples without walls. I haven't a clue how one prepares for the way of the Lord. I just know that when I was growing up and we were going to prepare for company, we slowed down, stocked the refrigerator and cleared the calendar. It's as simple as that.

Spiders

God has not given us a spirit of fear, But of power and love and of a sound mind. 2 timothy 1:7

Yesterday, Megan called for me with a note of panic in her voice. She called me to come to the bathroom to see a giant spider crawling on the shower curtain. When does it happen that I, a mere girl in my heart, have the courage to be the great protector and rid my children's lives of the creepy, crawly and the scary? At what age do we change from a young girl calling for help from her Momma and learn to reach up and rid our children's world of spiders ourselves? And why do I, Spider Eliminator extraordinaire, cease to rely on my own courage to reach my hand towards the black hairy creature when my husband is present?

Tapestry of life

Worthless scraps.
Torn, shredded fibers.
Add water.
Mix well.
Pour through a screen
Radiant beauty.
What remains is art in its true form,
Begotten, not made.
Creation.
The tapestry of life.

As water reflects a face, so a man's heart reflects the man.
Proverbs 27:19

Kari and I took a joy ride yesterday to Dawson, Minnesota. We went to the pottery and art studio of Tokheim Stoneware. The minute we saw the green rectangle of land holding a farmhouse, red barn and granary we could sense the cloak of peace that covered the place. It was so beautiful, loved, lived in and filled with spirit. We had seen some of the potters work at a small shop in Northfield but were not convinced of traveling to their studio because of the long drive. Curious about their open house, I called and spoke with Lucy. There was no choice after speaking with her that we must travel there. We were not disappointed.

It was so wonderful to breathe. It was wonderful to see a place like that existed. It was good to be invited into a stranger's home and be fully and completely, with heart and soul and works splayed wide open, invited in. We were invited in not only to see but also to be with. I will always remember their laughter and light, the way John stood on his legs so strongly, compact in his stable low to the ground strength. He stood in the room, hands clasped together, bright eyes lighting up space. His cautious quiet words spoke strength and welcome. He reminded me so much of my own father, a man radiant. I noticed the warmth and realized I was missing its presence. I haven't seen my Dad wearing this light recently; too often he hides, having been battered by the world. I miss this light on my Dad, the look of peace and contentment and joy, and the look of the Lord.

And Lucy, a beautiful wisp of a spirit, wise and seeing, I would love to sit down and hear her story. She paints. She sees. Can you imagine seeing a vision in your heart and following it, trusting enough to allow it to become? Can you imagine seeing a vision in your heart and using your hands to feel the call of clay? Can you imagine allowing your hands to be used as the vessel that helps to shape it? Perhaps the calling of an artist is not really a destination but a journey, a direction. Maybe it is more like truly seeing the quiet sunbeam of faith and hope and joy. Perhaps art, perhaps living is the ultimate sense of trusting of something greater than yourself. Perhaps it is allowing oneself to be fully vulnerable. Maybe it is in this spirit of humility that amazing things happen. Maybe then the finished piece is simply another marker on the journey of growing closer and closer to truth. Perhaps art dots our lives as glimpses of heaven in shapes of bowls, paintings, words, laughter, friends, children and parts of a life lived well.

I would love to visit again and sit by a window and listen to their story. I would love to hear where they have been and where they are going. How did they find the path? How do they continue to burn so brightly? I could listen to their heart and their eyes and know that I am not alone. I could listen and know this great big world is such a gift. God loves <u>all</u> his children so very much.

Julie Maijala Lundquist

"The Season of Giving"

Therefore consider carefully how you listen. Whoever has Will be given more; whoever does not have, even what he has will be taken from him. Luke 8:18

All the storefronts shout out as we approach the December holidays "Buy early, save at the Day After Thanksgiving Sale, and be sure to remember your hairdresser, post man, garbage collector"… And the list goes on. I will not dispute we are called to serve. I believe wholeheartedly we are created to give and to bless. What I am curious about is the receiving part.

Many of my friends make birthday cakes for Baby Jesus. "It is his birthday, after all." I can't argue with that. They throw birthday parties for Jesus complete with cake and ice cream and paper hats. It breaks my heart and I am not really sure why. Maybe I am sad because Jesus came to this world as a gift. God looked at his creation and loved us so very much that he sent his very own baby son. He sent this little tiny baby into our world as a living sacrifice for us. I get the reason to celebrate. I do see the side of this "season of giving." But I think first we must recognize that this is the "Season of Receiving."

It is the season of holding out our own hands and heart and accepting the baby Jesus into our life. It is the season of opening our hands and unwrapping this most precious gift –not tossing it aside, not asking for the receipt to return him because he wasn't quite the King we expected – wrong size, wrong family, too small. Maybe I am sad because we are rushing through the gift opening in order to get to the cake and ice cream part. I am not sure God intended for us to celebrate the birth of his most holy son with angel food cake and ice cream. I think what he really wants is for us to look into the manger, unwrap the gift and receive Him into our hearts as the newborn King. Halleluiah, Christ is born!

Rest in the Lord

They will build houses and dwell in them; They will plant vineyards and eat their fruit. Isaiah 65:21

One of my favorite memories of Christmas was going to the candlelight Christmas Eve service. Although it was held late and I often drifted in and out of sleep, it remains one of my most vivid memories, complete with sight, sound and smell. I remember sitting on old wooden pews, never quite comfortable, trying to get situated between my parents. The Maijala family typically entered the pew in this order, Dad, me, Mom, Kari. I can remember entering the dark sanctuary and resting in light given off by candles. Soon enough the music and voice of the pastor lulled me to sleep and I would drift off with my cheek on Dad or Mom's chest. I remember the way their hearts beat, their scent, and the sound of their breathing.

There was never another time quite like this, the one on Christmas eve, when I felt so protected, so full of trust and love and joy and absolute contentment that I would simply slide into sleep. It was the only time of the year that we knew we could simply drift off into sleep and everything would be all right. I suppose it is as close to heaven as the hallmark of our imagination gets, gentle music of praise and adoration, light from candles spilling warmth on faces pushing away darkness while the world focuses on the birth of our King and Savior. Perhaps this was truly God's hope that we so fully trust and believe in him that we rest completely in his arms, forever knowing He will never leave or forsake us.

Road trip

Driving 1200 miles to Montana has made me think about time. How often do I question time and travel. "How much longer? How much further? When will we get there? Are we almost there? It occurred to me that I feel those same questions regarding my spiritual journey.

As we were driving down the highway, I caught myself while forming the question "How much longer to Bozeman?" It was an interesting place to become aware - during the formation of a question. But it allowed me to question the question. Why do I really want to know how much longer? What will this knowledge give me? How will it influence my decisions? What does it matter?

I thought of early explorers and pioneers. I though of their endless days of travel before Google map. Can you imagine setting off on an adventure without really knowing the way? Imagine heading out for some glorious adventure in search of a natural wonder, a new home, or a different landscape without really knowing how long it would take to get there? Can you imagine traveling by heart and internal direction rather than by Google map and travel guide?

I caught a glimpse of idolatry of time in my life through this questioning. I see that I so often obey the clock. In essence, I worship time. I believe that I can't do something I want to do because I don't have enough time. I sometimes have placed so many constraints on my days that I become paralyzed and do not do anything that is my heart's desire (i.e.: read a book, draw, visit, walk the dog, go for a run, pray, have coffee with a friend, cook homemade soup, snuggle on the couch with my children, hold hands with my husband.) I realized I really wanted to know how much further we had to travel to our next stop because I wanted to know if I had enough time to. ...(Fill in the blank). I allowed the quantity of minutes available to make the decision for my action (or lack there of). But what if the amount of time we have, the number of miles left to travel, is less important than simply doing what we want to do.

What if we lived our lives more like an adventurer or pioneer on a journey? What if we lived trusting in a God so much bigger than ourselves (or the depths of knowledge in Google map) and followed our hearts to lead us on our journey? What if we stopped and rested along the banks of some amazing place simply because we saw the beauty, or heard the leaves rustling and decided we wanted to rest, not because of a set timeline or something a guidebook tells us we should, but because we realized the gift of the present moment. We realized stopping was what we <u>wanted</u> to do.

What if we traveled on our spiritual journey, what if we lived our lives this way? What if we saw each day, each moment as the gift it really is? What if we stopped looking at the clock and just traveled. What if we realized our whole life truly is just that – a journey without a timeline, but a journey with markers. Markers not telling us how many miles left to go, but instead is a life filled with sign posts telling us how far we have come? What if we lived our lives in anticipation, belief and trust our life is a constant learners journey, without a set endpoint, but a gift of unlimited growth and potential? What if the meaning of life is only found in the living?

So often I want to ask God "How much farther? How much more to learn till I get to a certain "level?" I sometimes struggle with wanting to rest on my laurels and quit paying so much attention to life. Sometimes I want to go back to living my unilluminated life. Sometimes I sound like a child asking, "Is this enough?" after they try only a bite of some food they are not so sure they like. Sometimes I want to ask God – how about this? Is this good enough? Am I done yet?

Then, in that very minute, I feel myself praying. I feel my heart and soul and body longing for more, hungering for growth, sight, wisdom and life that only God can teach. And I come before my God and ask for continued guidance and light. I ask God to renew my mind and my heart and my soul. I ask God to use my life.

I realize that we miss the point of living if we keep asking "how much farther." We miss a big part of the gift of God when we are focused only on the future and the past. We miss the joy of Lord, we miss our strength, and we miss our life. And, if we don't choose to journey, to travel, to learn, we will never ever experience the wonders that God has in store for us. If we as a people choose to remain slaves to the clock and the worldly calendar we miss the glorious places God wants to lead us. If we miss the journey, will we really ever have lived? If we miss the journey will we ever really find home?

Noble Character

Even the sparrow has found a home, and the swallow a nest for herself, where she may have her young – a place near your altar. O Lord Almighty, my King and my God. Blessed are those who dwell in your house; they are ever praising you. Psalm 84:3

I want to get out there and do something great, do something big. I want to make a difference. I am realizing that this way of thinking usually pulls me out of the present and makes me think that something else out there, apart from the life that is before me this very day, is what will matter. It is this thinking that removes me from the life, the gift at hand.

The story of Ruth tells us about a woman who is highly esteemed. She is a wife of noble character; it is her bloodline from Obed, Jesse and David that eventually leads to the birth of Christ. Ruth had no idea of knowing that the decisions that she made every day would have such long lasting, amazing effects on not only her life at the very present, but on all lives for future generations, even ours. Her story gives me great hope and encouragement to stay in the present. In gives me trust to believe that God's hand is at work in all the details, that God does indeed have a bigger picture in mind than we can ever fathom. It leads me to believe that I may never know, until the day of eternity, the true battles/ forces/ implications that my simple life of today may have for the kingdom.

Big Timber Rancher

Keep on loving each other as brothers. Do not forget to entertain strangers, for by doing so some people have entertained angels without knowing it. Hebrews 13:1-2

It's a little like the movie Ground Hog Day. Bill Murray wakens day after day to the same scene. Exactly one year ago to the date, we showed up in the Big Timber Country skillet. This morning, January 20th (Jake's birthday) the kids chose to sit at the exact same tables that we did last year – and so did we. We had already ordered when Jim walked in.

Jim Howe, slightly stooped, face still shiny from his morning wash walked over to the table next to us. As he sat down, I looked at him and asked him if he was indeed Jim Howe. He said , "yep – it's still the same name as last year." I don't quite think he could believe that we remembered his name – and honestly it made my heart jump because somewhere in his mind he remembered us, a rag tag family of travelers from one year ago. But Jim was someone you could meet once at a small town truck stop and never forget.

It saddened me to hear that his lovely wife died last summer, on June 21st. It must have been hard. Jim, a man of truth corrected me "It's being hard." No past tense about it – losing your wife. It's a loss that one lives with every day. From our two brief conversations it is clear to see that this is a man who clearly knows how to live. He credits his walk with the Lord. With a sparkle in his eye and a face that lights up like a steady beacon guiding the way, he shares snippets and stories about his wife, his family, his ranching, all the while chuckling about the joy of Lord. His words are like the laughter of a stream winding through rocks and thick roots growing exposed up from the bank. This morning the country Skillet made me weepy in that Hallmark commercial sort of way – only this wasn't some contrived, romantic clip, it was real truth, real living.

Jeremy was there, a young man of maybe 20, waiting on our family and children, writing down our orders as if he really heard what each of us wanted. He carried himself with confidence and I wondered how much longer this little town could hold him. Would he be wooed to the big city with offers of opportunity, cash and choices? Or will this young Jeremy be able to see the truth? Does he see the richness and the abundance right where he is? Does he already know the secret of living- that right where he is today is enough? Does he know, some place in his being, that this little two bit town is rich with laughter, and a rhythm of life that is clearly visible, a rhythm of life that while maybe being harder than many others, runs so much closer to the vein of truth? Does he know that the places with so much more "opportunity" certainly can be places of lives lived with truth, but there it is so often much harder to find. And most certainly, when it's hard to see – it's easy to get lost.

And the cook, another young kid flipping pancakes and French toast in the back with a black skullcap pulled low, barely touching black sunglasses resting on his face. His crooked smile and hearty grin glowed bright below, overpowering his black clothes. His body danced and weaved behind the stainless counter, moving to his own beat, punctuating the kitchen with laughter. Cleary this was a boy who knew how to live, could hear the groan of a heart, and knew how to work. Jim Howe walked into the restaurant and before he sat down they had a cup of hot coffee waiting for him. Without ordering, soon to follow came his breakfast.

I sat there in the booth at the Country Skillet and all around me I saw a slice of real living. This little town tucked outside the city limits of its big sister Livingston, seemed to me to be the true town of living. All around us we saw booths start out early with one or two folks, and as the sun rose higher more people came and joined in sharing stories and breakfast with their neighbors. The whole place breathed with hearty laughter and conversation. I wonder what it would be like to grow up in a place that you could really call home. How has it happened that our house number in the suburbs has so often become our only home? What happened to rich true community – a community where you treated other folks with respect and value because they were part of your family? What would it be like to have fewer choices of places to frequent so relationships were actually made? What would it be like to live somewhere that was so in tune with the details of who you were that when you walked in the door you were greeted with a smile, a cup of hot coffee and already knew your order?

"The good Lord says that laughter is the best medicine." "Don't ever let the sun go down with any anger between you." "The easiest way not to get caught in a lie is to tell the truth." Jim Howe insists that he and his wife never argued. They disagreed, yes, but they were able to share laughter and they never went to bed angry. He spoke highly of his three children, his 11 grand children and 4 great grand children. How amazed he and his wife were, that all this had begun with just the two of them.

Jim believes in always speaking the truth, that way you don't ever have to try and remember what you said. I asked for his address –and said that I would like to send him cards…do you like to write? The truth is, he doesn't like to write, but he sure likes getting letters. How refreshing is that? He spoke about his wife and him losing a baby girl. The doctor told him that there was no way his wife should ever try to have another baby or else Jim might lose her. So, they adopted a baby girl three weeks old. He paused and continued the story by saying that she still is Daddy's little sweetie even today. He can't imagine living without her loving on him.

A Lot of Living

Whether you go to the right or to the left, your ears will hear a voice behind you, saying, "This is the way; walk in it."
Isaiah 30:21

I called Dad on the way home just to check in and see how he and Mom were doing. It was good to hear his voice and even better to hear his heart speak. I asked how his week had been and he told me he had done a lot of living this week. The truth of those words took me by surprise. How is it that over the past few days this writing has been an ongoing dialogue of truth and living for everyone in my life? I asked Dad what " a lot of living" means. His answer made me smile. "Going for walks, ice skating on the pond behind the house, seeing a great movie with Mom Saturday night." Sounds like Dad struck the vein of living. It's the quiet pulse that really cries out to be heard. It's the pulse that beats in the heart and soul and calls to us like the quiet of wind rustling through grass. It the voice of One calling out to us, loving us. It is the matter of life and death.

Leadership

I must admit, my prideful ego had grand and lofty ideas about what it meant to be a leader. In all honesty, I believe the truth is that we are called in leadership wherever God has planted us each and every day.

2 Kings has a great story about Elisha. The leper travels a great distance for healing. Elisha, a man of God, commands the leper to simply wash in the river seven times. Seven, the number of perfection, of completeness of wholeness. The leper becomes outraged because surely something as simple as washing in the stream could never cure him. Interestingly, it is the man's servant that points out that his master, the leper, would indeed have done "anything" to get cured, so why wasn't simply washing in the river good enough?

The story is a good illustration of the backward thinking we often have regarding important issues. When I apply the story to the topic of leadership, I see that true leadership is quite opposite of the ideas I grew up with. I had always thought of a leader as one who had all the answers. They were the ones who knew right from wrong, and certainly knew exactly where I should be heading. But in truth, a good leader must be a follower. A good leader, by very nature, will shine out because they are indeed simply reflecting the light of their truth, their values, of God. A good leader gets out of the way and encourages each member in their community to follow their call, to speak their voice, to come out and play. A good leader shows up with intent to life. A good leader chooses to engage – to be open and honest and to listen. A good leader is not afraid of healthy discourse. A good leader knows that they, too, are on a learner's journey and lead as a leader/follower. A good leader encourages and builds up. A good leader does not blow smoke, or give "Pollyanna" compliments – but is truthful, honest, open and sincere. A good leader is not afraid of silence and chooses to make silence a member of the community, knowing full well that God's voice is indeed a quiet whisper.

A good leader engages not because they think they have all the answers, but they know that by freeing their own voice, they will free another's. A good leader knows that she must speak not because she if afraid that if she doesn't, Gods work won't get done – but because she knows that God created us so uniquely that when we speak our truths, we are filled with peace and joy, love and compassion. A good leader knows that this life is a true gift, and every member must be welcomed in. A good leader knows the importance of meeting people exactly where they are at, and calling out the goodness that surrounds them not by telling answers, but by asking questions. A good leader knows the value of servant hood, for indeed the greatest will become the least, and the least the greatest.

So, our role? I believe it is to live out our faith in community with others, to indeed, grow together. Not to only admit that this is a journey that we are all on, but to fully embrace the uniqueness of each and encourage others to let their lights shine. You don't just cross a finish line and get in. We are called to believe that the kingdom of God is near, now and live as beginners in faith every day. We are asked to live our lives in service, not as a payback, but out of the joyful gratitude that fills our heart to be a part of a group of followers trying to learn how to put our faith into form.

Julie Maijala Lundquist

She's Hard on Her Shoes

And how shall they preach unless they are sent? As it is written: "How beautiful are the feet of those who preach the gospel of peace, who bring tidings of good things!" Romans 10:14-15

I have never been able to keep a pair of shoes looking good very long. As a matter of fact, my feet are usually in pretty rough shape too. I thought that perhaps my battered shoes and feet were a reflection of lack of care on my part. So, I treated myself last spring to a French manicure on my toes. You know, sandal season and all that. I got myself a beautiful French manicure and hopped on a plane heading south. My destination? Guatemala. Have you ever seen French manicured toes that have been walking hard all day in dust and dirt? Believe me, it was awful. I felt like a teenage girl who put on way too much make up trying to be pretty, and instead created an eye sore. I was caught wearing a façade of beauty on my toes. I realized as I looked down at ugly white nail polish that I would rather stand strong in true naked beauty than be hiding behind perfectly manicured toes.

Being hard on our shoes, hard on our feet means that we are in motion. It means that we are traveling, spreading the tidings of good things wherever we go. It means moving, jumping, falling, playing and living!!! What a blessing. Beautiful feet tell the story of the LORD. In Guatemala, I saw an old woman, barefoot, walking through the town as she carried a bowl of ground corn like a crown on her head. Her feet were worn, calloused and rough. She certainly had never had a pedicure, probably had never soaked her feet in a tub, maybe even never had rubbed her soles with lotion, yet they were translucent with beauty. She carried herself tall and proud, with humility and grace, radiance shining forth. I wonder where her feet had carried her, who they had traveled with, the steps she had taken from the time she was a young child skipping and twirling, to the steps of an old woman, shuffling through the town, head high. She was simply beautiful.

View

By wisdom a house is built and through understanding it is established; through knowledge its rooms are filled with rare and beautiful treasures. Proverbs 24:3

Maybe the view we look for isn't really outside our windows at all. Maybe the view that we see when we are truly living our life isn't the beauty that is outside the windows of our heart. True beauty is what is inside our heart and soul. True beauty is living our own life full with spirit – and suddenly everything is illuminated with beauty. Perhaps natural beauty that surrounds us – in nature, music, art, people – is simply the reflection of the truth of beauty within.

May your life be dedicated to beauty - it's truth and reflection. May your life hold voices, images, dreams, love and memories of discovery of this amazing life you have been given.

Julie Maijala Lundquist

Patience

By standing firm you will gain life. Luke 21:19

I always thought that patience had to do with sitting and waiting. It really doesn't – but it looks like that because true patience is centered, like when throwing a pot. When you first start on the wheel you throw your clay down and center the lump. You know that it is centered when it is no longer banging and bumping, when it is no longer thrashing from side to side. When it is centered, it feels still – but if you open your eyes, it is moving. Patience really has nothing to do with waiting and sitting around. It has everything to do with moving and faith. We must take action and trust God has indeed begun a plan and is working. It has to do with knowing what you have hoped for has already begun. Patience is more about giving up control of the timetable and trusting that things are progressing. It is not about being still. It is life that is living and moving and breathing, centered on truth.

In Luke, when Jesus is praying, the disciples ask him to teach them how to pray. Jesus tells them the story of the man who needs three loaves of bread for his neighbor who comes knocking on his door late one night. Praying isn't about sitting on your hands and hoping. It is about getting up in the middle of the night and banging on doors. It is about taking action. We must ask and believe God is indeed working now, already, this very minute. Patience is all about believing that God's work has already begun. Jesus tells this story about asking – not just verbally, but physically – and at all hours.

Who Are We Trying To Save?

I have been really thinking about those words lately. Who are we trying to save? It seems to be a phrase that comes up over and over again. Why are we reaching out and targeting the unchurched? Who are they? I get stressed and feel confined whenever I hear these words.

I must say that I don't believe we can save – only God does. Perhaps my guff doesn't have anything to do with the "wanting to share the message of Jesus" part. I can't be against that because that is how I try to live my life. I pray for help to love God before all else and love my neighbors and enemies as myself. Too often the "bringing people to Jesus" rhetoric is filled with superiority and "my way or the highway" conversation. I personally choose the highway. I often wonder if it is driven from one's ego. How often do we hear "I am right about this Jesus and unless you (insert whatever theme you want) go to church, don't have sex before marriage, serve, etc. you will not be saved."? I am not sure about any of those judgment calls. I am sure that the word of God says over and over to LOVE all – not convert, argue, or make others feel smaller or lesser, but to love all.

Maybe what I am saying is that I really do agree with evangelism. I agree that I need to live my life fully and wholly and Christ centered. I know that living this way is how my life has been constantly changed and transformed every step of the way. I trust that God is much bigger than me and that he has great works in mind. I believe that he does and will lead us into paths of others everyday that we can learn from – and maybe teach something to. But the majority of our "story", perhaps the most important part of our story as Christians needs to be how we live our lives each and every day.

Too often I hear Christians living lives out of scarcity, hate, non-tolerance and exclusivity. These are the very devises that will continue to divide us. It is not until we are willing to stand together in the great truth of knowing that God created each and every one of us as unique individuals with gifts and abilities – and stand and encourage one another in love that we will really be able to get things done. That means forgetting about the numbers, the notches on the lipstick case, and knowing that every person you see – on the streets, at work, in school – is indeed one of God's precious children.

What if we choose our words last and our actions first to tell the most amazing story ever told? What if we forget about bringing Christ to the world artificially and instead consider living our own lives with Christ in the center? What if we consider a much more organic approach to Christianity? Some days that might mean acts of simple kindness, other times it might mean sharing our own story about how we have gone from knowing Christ with our heads to knowing Christ with our heart. I know I will never be an expert on right living. I only know that I must choose everyday to live with intent following in the way of Jesus. Most times I fail. But the only story I find worth telling is simple: Jesus loves me … and you. This I know.

Obedience

I was thinking about people who have many different gifts. Some people try their hand at something new – and pull things off pretty well. There is a lot of courage in trying new things. There is a lot of courage in being a beginner. Once you have tried something new it is even easier to try others things. The learning just seems to stack up on itself and the curve seems to shorten.

If we have a child who is readily "good" or "natural" at many things, how can we encourage him? Our culture teaches that if you are good at something, stick with it. But what if you are good at a number of things (and I think we all are – or would be if we were willing to try something new). How realistic is that? I don't believe that doing it all is the answer. If we follow the advice of the world we will fail miserably from exhaustion or miss out on the very things that we *want* to do. Maybe even what we want to do will cause us to work hard and practice in order to be. When I think of the stuff that I love to do, most of the things at the top of my list are things that I have to work very hard at.

No matter what, we need to teach each other to listen to what our hearts want. If we ask ourselves "why" we want to do something, the answer can help us clarify our intent. If our children say that they want to take a break from or quit something they are good at, too often I hear our society say NO! You can't do that. We are often afraid that even if we step back from something to take a closer look at what we really want we will lose ground. We are afraid we will never amount to anything if we don't hold on to a worthless scrap as we listen to what other's say about us. This is a fear-based answer. If we do one thing as teachers, parents and friends, we must direct our companions to listen. We need to teach each other to ask and listen and then trust that God is and will be guiding us our entire life. If we don't listen to our children when they speak to us from their hearts, why would <u>they</u> ever listen? Wouldn't we be teaching them that the small quiet voice doesn't matter?

If my child, a good soccer player, chooses not to play anymore I must trust that God has something much greater in store for him. I know that it takes a lot of courage to leave something that you are good at. When we are good at something we get lots of kudos, are highly visible and well known. We must ask why he wants to take a break. They may not be able to articulate an answer – but perhaps he will find the freedom in his heart. Maybe he will find the space that he needs when he realizes that what he hears there matters.

I think that this is what obedience is really about. I know that sometimes God's will and my egotistical will are at odds. There is a spot where it is ego vs. truth. I believe that God dwells within each one of us and if we ask and listen we will always be guided. I know that this world isn't about an egotistical me, I believe God created each one of us unique. It is not until we start listening to God speak that we will really be able to get some things done here on earth.

Rooftops

So the people went out and brought back branches and built themselves booths on their own roofs, in their courtyards, in the courts of the house of God and in the square by the Water Gate and on by the Gate of Ephraim. The whole company that had returned from exile built booths and lived in them. From the days of Joshua son of Nun until that day, the Israelites had not celebrated it like this. And their joy was very great.
Nehemiah 9:16-17

Think of a puzzle with many different pieces. Each piece holds a unique image that is essential in building the entire picture. Think how important it is for each piece to come together for completion. Think of how important is it for us to come together to live and celebrate life.

What if the map of heaven, the markers and the guides is something like a puzzle and on each of our hands is carved a portion. What if it is not until we all come together in love for one another that God's glory can be seen? What if the map of heaven carved in the palms of our hands is waiting for us to realize that loving one's neighbor and enemy is not a suggestion, but the only true action in the fulfillment of the Kingdom of God? What if the map of heaven is carved in the palm of our hands and we have been blind to it all these years because we have been too stubborn and stiff-necked to look down? What if the map of heaven is carved in the palm of our hands and only by opening our fists we experience the joy of giving and receiving? What if God's kingdom multiplies when we stand together, palms outstretched reaching toward the heavens? What if it really is as simple as washing in the river seven times?

Epiphany

If I am prayer about making a decision and ask for guidance and then choose to say yes to something and I sit with the decision, I may feel joyful and at peace. Still prayerful I know that this is a right thing for me and I will continue on this path.

If I am prayerful about making a decision and ask for guidance and choose to say yes and I sit with the decision, and after I make the decision am not at peace and I feel tight and constrained. Still prayerful, I know that this is not the right thing for me and I need to step back and say no.

Being prayerful and walking with God does not mean that I will never change my mind about a decision. It is more important to honor my spirit than to believe that things can't or won't change. Being prayerful and walking with God does not mean that I will not make mistakes. Being prayer and following in the Way means that I must quiet myself and listen and trust that God will always guide me. Being prayerful and walking with God means that I will disappoint others sometimes.

Walking with God means that when I ask and listen and am given guidance, I must continue to be compassionate with myself. Walking with God means learning the (painful) art of saying no. Walking with God means knowing that I am not the answer – it means that God is and he must always come first.

Follower

In Matthew the four fishermen leave everything behind and follow Jesus. I have always read this and thought of following Jesus and following church as the same thing. Perhaps it is not. I opened the gospel to this story today in Matthew and am wondering if I am selfish and not willing to leave everything and follow Jesus.

When I read this story in Matthew before I heard – Jesus wants you to quit your job and work for the church. I may have heard Jesus wants you to sell everything and be a missionary in the fields of Africa. I may have heard this story is telling me to quit my job and drop everything and go into ministry. I heard it and thought that Jesus may be calling me to tell me I should go to seminary so I can be a pastor. But today, for the first time I see that the disciples aren't really leaving. They are fishermen before they meet Jesus – and will continue to be. Yes, they will have a different catch, but they indeed remain fishermen. They are to give up the old way of fishing for the only way.

Maybe that is what we are to do. Leave the comfort and trappings of our old life and leadership to simply follow Jesus. Maybe it really is about simply following Jesus – and I have followed him all my life in the church (actively, wholeheartedly in the church) – but perhaps now he is leading me through the church, beyond the walls, the dogma, the programming, the projects, the rules, the church calendar, the doing – to freedom and the living well.

Perhaps the nets and boats that the four fishermen leave represent their past way of living. Maybe it signifies the trust we put in our possessions and ourselves. They leave all they know to follow Jesus. Perhaps when we truly follow Jesus we learn that we don't need nets, we need love. We don't need boats, we need belief. Perhaps the nets and the boat are simply used to illustrate anything that traps us or keeps us from trusting in this amazing God and his amazing Son.

In the gospels Jesus talks about "trappings" that can be roadblocks in following him. Some of them include: Nets, Boats, Father, Time,

Unbelief, Money, Home, Brothers, Sisters, Mothers, Children, and Fields. All these can hinder us from following Jesus and finding the kingdom.

A Letter To You

Dear One,

It fills my heart with great joy to know that you will be receiving this letter. The richness, depth and breadth of this life is a wonderful gift. Cherish, honor it and respect it. There is no place for fear in this world – only compassion and love. Relish life and in those around you – see the light shining in their faces, see the awesomeness of creation. Walk with the One you know. Listen for the questions and listen for the answers. For you hold all you need and all you have ever needed. Knock at the door and fight with all your power to keep it open. Many would like to have it shut but those that love you will guide you to places and things as true as the unending sky above and the reflection of sun dancing across water.

You are indeed wonderfully made. Remember to play and splash and sing and laugh. Remember to live well. Love your babies and your family and your neighbors and your enemies wholly and completely. Keep the surface of your heart dusted by receiving the cleansing of the great wind that blows around you.

Tears are good, like rain drenching dry fields. Do not be afraid of them. I let them fall even as I write this knowing full well with faith and hope and trust that the blooms in your garden will be amazing. Simply trust. I hold you as gently as a bird in the palm of my hand.

Get outside of yourself and love every person you meet. Fear not, for you are never alone. Know that my guidance is there always. I will never let you go. Give thanks and praise in all you do. For life is a gift created for you.

Peace to you, joy and love. Oh so much love.

Julia Maijala Luundquist is available for speaking engagements and personal appearances. For more information contact:

Julia Maijala Luundquist
C/O Advantage Books
P.O. Box 160847
Altamonte Springs, Florida 32716

To purchase additional copies of this book or other books published by Advantage Books call our toll free order number at:
1-888-383-3110 (Book Orders Only)

or visit our bookstore website at:
www.advbookstore.com

Longwood, Florida, USA
"we bring dreams to life"™
www.advbooks.com

Printed in the United States
100208LV00004B/1-99/A

9 781597 551328